Tony & Chris Grogan

A Dales High Way
Companion

2018
Published by Skyware Ltd.

Published in 2018 by
Skyware Ltd.
48 Albert Avenue
Saltaire, Shipley BD18 4NT
www.skyware.co.uk

ISBN 978-1-911321-00-2

© Tony & Chris Grogan 2018
First published by Skyware Ltd. 2009.

Chris grew up on a hill farm in Dentdale. Tony grew up in Shipley on the edge of the moors. Both now live in Saltaire.

All rights reserved. No part of this book may be reproduced in any form or by any means without permission in writing from the publisher.

Route maps based on OS Opendata. Contains Ordnance Survey data © Crown copyright and database right 2017.

British Library Cataloguing-in-Publication Data.
A catalogue record for this book is available from the British Library.

Every care has been taken in the preparation of this book and all the information has been carefully checked and is believed to be correct at the time of publication. However, the countryside changes and neither the authors nor the publishers can accept responsibility for any errors or omissions or for any loss, damage, injury or inconvenience resulting from the use of this book.

Also from Skyware Press: **A Dales High Way: Route Guide**. A practical pocket guide, with full colour strip maps at a scale of 1:25,000, comes in a handy weather resistant plastic wallet. Available via the website.

Cover photo: Malham Cove. Title Page photo: Crossing the northern Howgill Fells. Opposite page photo: Gordale Scar (photo © Jacob Lyons).

Printed by Briggs Bros (Silsden) Ltd, Cononley Business Park, Cononley, West Yorkshire.

Acknowledgements

A special thanks to **Julia Pearson** for her help in compiling and writing the wildlife sections.

We are grateful for the help and advice of many people, including Alison Armstrong, Amy Ball (*Craven Museum & Gallery*), Keith Boughey, Richard Cann (*Sedbergh & District History Society*), Ellie Clement, Gavin Edwards, Matt Hannam, Bridget Izod, Alan King, Yvonne Luke, Jo Mackintosh (*Cumbria County Council*), David Marchant (*East Riding of Yorkshire Council Museums*), Ian Murdoch, Elizabeth Parkin (*Fell Pony Society*), Mark Rand (*Friends of the Settle-Carlisle Line*) and John Steel (*Cumberland & Westmorland Antiquarian & Archaeological Society*). Thanks also to Che Grogan & Kel Shackleton.

For permission to reproduce their photos we thank: Neil Aldridge, John Bridges, Eliza & John Forder, Simon Leddingham, Jacob Lyons, Julia Pearson, David Pratt, Dave Ryall and Pete Shaw.

Many of the wildlife photographs are taken from John Bridges' excellent North East Wildlife website. All wildlife photos marked (*N.E.W.*) are © **www.northeastwildlife.co.uk** whilst those marked (JP) are © Julia Pearson.

Other photos and images reproduced courtesy of the Craven Museum & Gallery, English Heritage, the Sunday Mirror and the Yorkshire Dales National Park Authority. Public Domain images come mostly from Wikimedia Commons (http://commons.wikimedia.org). All other photos are those of the authors, their family and friends.

The original route was devised with help and advice from the Countryside and Rights of Way officers of Cumbria County Council, North Yorkshire County Council, Bradford Metropolitan District Council and the Yorkshire Dales National Park.

Finally a special thanks to the good folk at our local printers - Briggs Bros (Silsden) Ltd. To have such helpful, patient and talented people on your doorstep is a real bonus.

APPLEBY-IN-WESTMORLAND

Great Asby

Kirkby Stephen

Newbiggin-on-Lune

SECTION 6
EDEN VALLEY
Newbiggin-on-Lune to Appleby
(12.7 miles)

Sedbergh

Settle to Carlisle railway

SECTION 5
HOWGILL FELLS
Sedbergh to Newbiggin-on-Lune
(10.9 miles)

Dent

Garsdale

Yorkshire Dales National Park

Chapel-le-Dale

Ribblehead

SECTION 4
DENTDALE
Chapel-le-Dale to Sedbergh
(15.7 miles)

Horton-in-Ribblesdale

Stainforth

Settle

SECTION 3
INGLEBOROUGH
Settle to Chapel-le-Dale
(14.2 miles)

Long Preston

Malham

Hellifield

Hetton

Gargrave

Skipton

SECTION 2
MALHAMDALE
Skipton to Settle
(18.7 miles)

Addingham

Ilkley

Keighley

Bingley

SECTION 1
ROMBALDS MOOR
Salraire to Skipton
(17.9 miles)

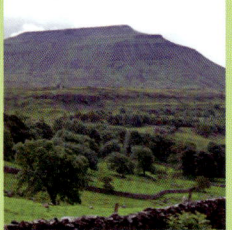

SALTAIRE Shipley

Contents

Acknowledgements 3
The Route 4
Contents 5
Introduction 6
Geology of the Dales...**8**; A Timeline of the Dales...**10**; Wildlife of the Dales...**11**;
Saltaire...**12**; Saltaire Map...**13**; Saltaire – World Heritage Site...**14**.

SECTION 1: ROMBALDS MOOR 17

Saltaire to Weecher Reservoir...**18**; Optional Route via Hope Hill...**19**; Geology...**20**; Ilkley...**21**; Weecher Reservoir to White Wells...**22**; White Wells to Addingham Moorside...**23**; Prehistoric Rock Art on Rombalds Moor...**24**; Addingham Moorside to Draughton Height...**26**; Addingham...**26**; Wildlife...**28**; Draughton Height to Skipton...**30**; Skipton...**31**.

SECTION 2: MALHAMDALE 33

Skipton to Sharp Haw...**34**; The Brigantes and the Roman Occupation...**35**; The Flasby Sword...**37**; Sharp Haw to Moor Lane (Hetton)...**38**; Rough Haw Enclosure...**38**; Wildlife...**40**; Moor Lane (Hetton) to Gordale House...**42**; Gordale House to Kirkby Fell...**43**; Geology...**44**; Kirkby Fell to Settle...**46**; Settle...**46**; The Caves of Attermire...**47**.

SECTION 3: INGLEBOROUGH 49

Settle to Smearset Scar...**50**; Smearset Scar to Crummack...**51**; Geology...**52**; Crummack to Simon Fell...**54**; Alternative bad weather route to Ribblehead and Hill Inn (Chapel-le-Dale)...**55**; Ingleborough Hillfort...**58**; Wildlife...**60**; Simon Fell to Hill Inn (Chapel-le-Dale)...**62**; Angles and Vikings...**63**.

SECTION 4: DENTDALE 65

Hill Inn (Chapel-le-Dale) to Blea Moor Sidings...**66**; Blea Moor Sidings to Wold End...**67**; Optional route over Whernside...**67**; Fell Running...**69**; Wold End to Dent...**70**; Dent to Longstone Fell...**71**; Dent...**71**; Wildlife...**72**; Longstone Fell to Sedbergh...**74**; The Harrying of the North...**75**; Adam Sedgwick...**76**; The Dent Fault...**77**; The Changing Dales...**78**.

SECTION 5: HOWGILL FELLS 81

Sedbergh to the Calf...**82**; Civil War and the Quakers...**83**; Geology...**85**; The Calf to West Fell...**86**; West Fell to Newbiggin-on-Lune...**87**; Enclosures...**87**; Fell Ponies...**88**; Alternative bad weather route from Sedbergh to Newbiggin-on-Lune via Cautley and Ravenstonedale...**90**; The English Monks...**91**.

SECTION 6: EDEN VALLEY 93

Newbiggin-on-Lune to Great Kinmond...**94**; Great Kinmond to Great Asby...**94**; Masongill Hut Circle Settlement...**95**; Wildlife...**96**; Great Asby to Hoff...**98**; Hoff to Appleby...**99**; Geology...**101**; Appleby-in-Westmorland...**102**; Lady Anne Clifford...**103**; Appleby Map...**104**; The Settle-Carlisle Railway...**106**; The Return Journey...**108**.

Index of Places...**110**; Select Bibliography...**112**.

INTRODUCTION

We first walked the route of **A Dales High Way** in September 2007.

From the historic mill village of Saltaire the route heads north, following ancient trade routes and green lanes wherever possible. It covers some of the most beautiful scenery in the Yorkshire Dales, crossing Rombalds Moor, with its mysterious prehistoric rock carvings, to reach the dramatic limestone scars of Malhamdale.

It climbs mighty Ingleborough - the Hollow Mountain - and crosses the Howgill Fells in a breathtaking six-mile ridge walk. Finally, after passing the isolated splendour of Sunbiggin Tarn, the walk finishes in Appleby, in the heart of the Eden Valley.

The walking is over but there is one final highlight to come - a return journey through the landscape just walked, on the spectacular Settle-Carlisle railway.

This long distance walk was officially launched in 2008 with the publication of the original **Route Guide**. It very quickly proved popular with walkers.

A Dales High Way however, is more than just a walk. It's a journey through place and time. **A Dales High Way Companion** is the story of that journey. It includes a detailed description of the route which, with the appropriate OS maps, is all you will need to navigate the way. More importantly though, it explores the fascinating geology, history, culture and wildlife of the places visited.

It is designed to help you get maximum enjoyment from your walk, whether it's finding rock art carved by our Stone Age ancestors, spotting an early purple orchid or visiting the best preserved medieval castle in England.

This book complements the **Route Guide** and is best read alongside it. The numbered reference points on the **Route Guide's** colourful strip maps are reflected in the paragraph numbers in the **Companion's** text.

The route itself divides naturally into six sections: Rombalds Moor, Malhamdale, Ingleborough, Dentdale, the Howgill Fells and the Eden Valley.

Seasoned walkers might tackle one section each day, but most people will find the first two sections too long. It is better to break them and take time to explore.

Accommodation is generally plentiful except perhaps at Chapel-le-Dale, so book there first or head for Ribblehead. Staying at

Looking east from Ingleborough

Ribblehead (pub or bunkbarn) adds an extra 1.9 miles on day five but saves 2.7 miles the following day.

For details of accommodation please check **A Dales High Way** website (*www.daleshighway.org.uk*), which also carries reported route changes, suggested itineraries, a news section and a walkers' forum.

Several baggage carriers such as **Brigantes** now service the route (details on website) and for a modest fee they will transfer your bags between stops, giving you the freedom to enjoy each day's walking carrying only a day bag. They can also offer a full holiday service, arranging and booking accommodation for the entire walk.

A compass and map are essential, even if you are carrying a GPS and mobile phone; batteries fail and signals disappear.

Most of the route is covered by two maps: OL2 and OL19. Unfortunately parts of Section 1 are covered by two others; the most useful is Explorer 297, with the first two miles covered by Explorer 288.

This book includes alternative bad weather routes for the highest sections, Ingleborough and the Howgill Fells.

The high terrain covered by the walk is exposed and it can be very cold and wet on the fell tops, even in summer. Bad weather and thick mist can descend quickly, so be well prepared and you'll be safe.

Always tell someone your plans and when to expect you back, especially if you walk alone.

The route sticks mostly to established rights of way but in a few places follows well-used tracks across open access land. Occasionally, in case of fire risk for example, restrictions may be imposed on these parts. Please follow suggested or obvious diversions.

Don't underestimate the challenging nature of this walk. There is a total ascent of 4.6 kilometres involved. Add in the optional route over Whernside and you have a climb equivalent to Mont Blanc, the highest mountain in western Europe!

Since ancient times people have climbed up to the high places, have built their homes there, their settlements, their religious monuments. Modern walkers have developed a habit of picking up stones and building cairns. However innocent the intention, it's a habit that needs to be broken. It is important that these places are left intact, for future generations to discover and reinterpret. Please tread lightly. As the saying goes, **take only photographs, leave only footprints**.

So, get out the maps, dust off the backpack, polish the boots. It's time to prepare for a great adventure: 90 miles across the glorious high country of the Yorkshire Dales, and back on England's most beautiful railway.

Much more than just a walk…

The walk can be conveniently undertaken in eight days, say Saturday to Saturday, with plenty of time then to enjoy the market towns and villages on the way.

Day 1: Saltaire to Ilkley	(7.5 miles)
Day 2: Ilkley to Skipton	(11.4 miles)
Day 3: Skipton to Malham	(12.9 miles)
Day 4: Malham to Stainforth	(10.3 miles)
Day 5: Stainforth to Chapel-le-Dale	(11.6 miles)
Day 6: Chapel-le-Dale to Sedbergh	(15.7 miles)
Day 7: Sedbergh to Newbiggin-on-Lune	(10.9 miles)
Day 8: Newbiggin-on-Lune to Appleby	(12.7 miles)

The total of 93 miles above includes diversions into Ilkley, Malham and Stainforth.

Geology of the Dales

The characteristic landscape features of the Dales and Eden Valley are ultimately influenced by the underlying bedrocks.

The rocks of the region are almost all sedimentary in nature, formed from materials deposited by wind or in water - on the sea bed or in river flood plains. They were later turned into rock through burial and compression.

The bedrocks are exposed in some places, like the limestone pavements of Malhamdale. Elsewhere they are buried under soil and glacial clays, such as the rolling fields of the Eden Valley.

Most of the region's rocks were laid down in the Carboniferous Period, just a relatively short span between 300 and 360 million years ago, when the area lay near the equator, under a shallow, tropical sea. This period is so named because most of the coal was formed during this time - nature's own method of carbon capture. The older Silurian and Ordovician rocks are denser and harder than their Carboniferous equivalents.

Sedimentary rocks are deposited in stratified beds. The main types to be found are:

Shale, Mudstone and Siltstone: these are formed from deposits of very fine muddy material which settle in horizontal layers, or laminations. Shale, the most common bedrock, tends to split and flake and is easily eroded when exposed to the weather. Under conditions of extreme pressure and heat, finer shales form **slate**.

Sandstone: this is formed from fine sandy deposits. The youngest rock in the region is the red sandstone of the Eden Valley. Sandstone formed from coarser grains is called **gritstone**, which caps the tops of the Three Peaks and covers the moorland hills.

Greywacke is a sandstone containing a mixture of various sized particles, including a large proportion of fine-grained rock. Found in Crummack Dale and the Howgills.

Limestone: a "living" rock, formed from shells and the broken down bodies of tiny, limey marine organisms deposited on the sea bed. The Great Scar Limestone, almost pure calcium carbonate, shows as huge, white terraces north of Malham.

Some rock series are given their own names and may have different rock types:

Yoredale Series: the name for a cyclic sequence of rocks that underlie almost half the Dales National Park. It consists of repeated layers of limestone, sandstone and shale. Produced when the sea level rose and fell again and again over a period of time, it sits on top of the Great Scar Limestone and makes up the body of the Three Peaks.

Millstone Grit: a sequence of sandstones (mostly hard, coarse gritstone) and shales. Produced by a huge, expanding river delta that fed the shallow sea covering Yorkshire around 300 million years ago. Forms much of the upland Pennine moors. The coarse gritstone, once used for making millstones, is also popularly known as *millstone grit*.

Coal Measures: this is another sequence of rocks, mainly sandstone and shale, with thin layers of coal making up about 5% of the total. It was produced as large areas of forest were repeatedly flooded. Found mainly to the south of the region, such as Baildon Moor, it was a very important economic resource.

Deeply underlying these bedrocks in much of the National Park area is a huge slab of granite, forming a fairly stable landmass called the Askrigg Block. Earthquakes and land movements have left this block largely unaffected, but at its edges long fault-lines have appeared, where the earth has been uplifted or dropped. To the south are the Craven Faults and to the west the Dent Fault. They mark dramatic and sudden changes in the visible landscape.

More recently the land has been scoured and carved by great ice sheets. The last ice age period, or glaciation, began around 80,000 years ago. During that time ice covered all of this region, carving the former river valleys into wide, U-shaped glacial valleys and exposing the vast limestone pavements.

GEOLOGY OF THE DALES & EDEN VALLEY

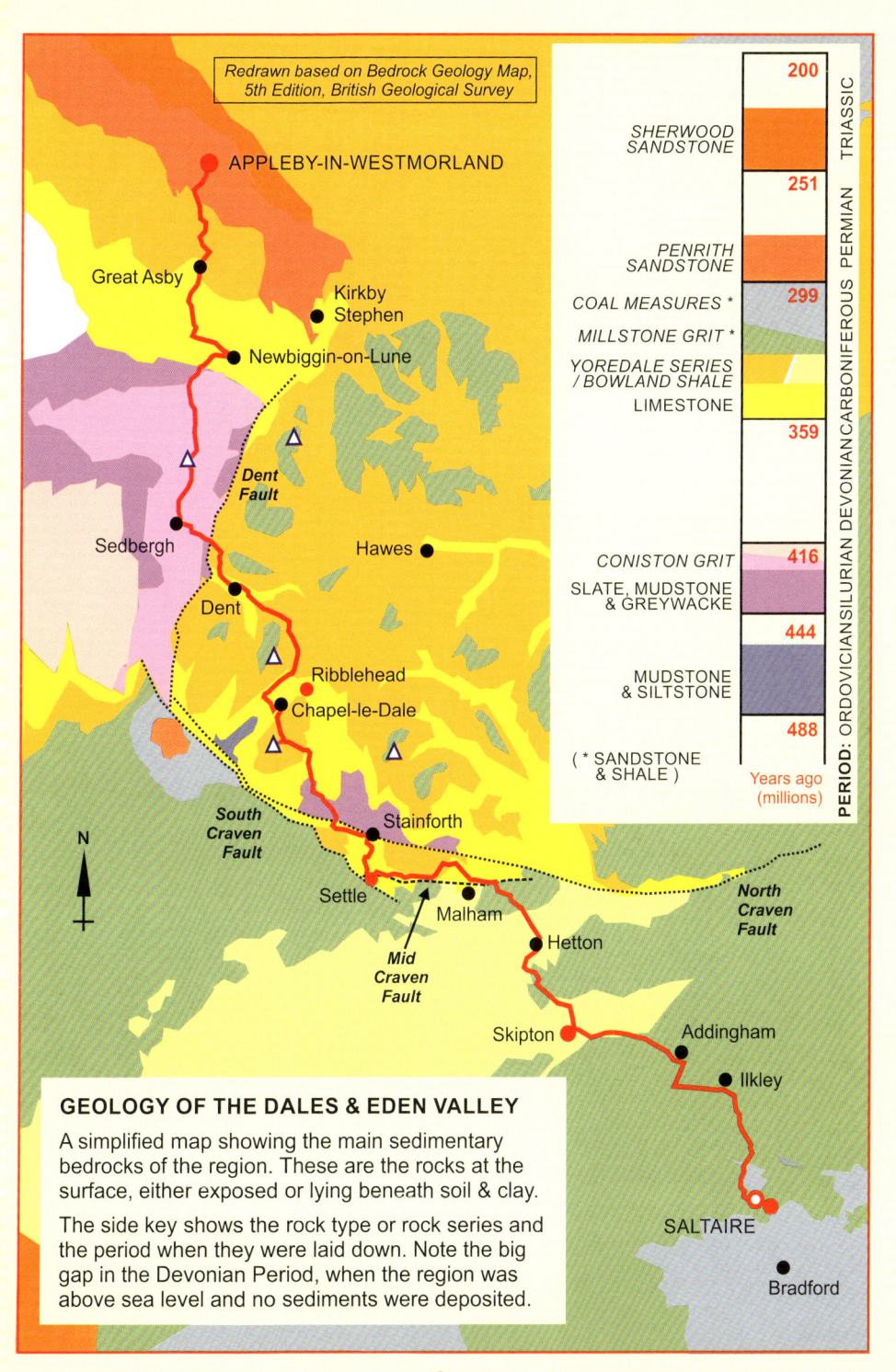

A simplified map showing the main sedimentary bedrocks of the region. These are the rocks at the surface, either exposed or lying beneath soil & clay.

The side key shows the rock type or rock series and the period when they were laid down. Note the big gap in the Devonian Period, when the region was above sea level and no sediments were deposited.

A Timeline of the Dales

The landscape you see today has been radically altered by human occupation. The bleak upland areas would have been covered in woodland 6,000 years ago, and without people and grazing sheep they would soon revert to woodland.

A Dales High Way is a walk through time. In each section you will find accounts of historical artefacts and sites that can be seen along the route. Below is a simple timeline with some of those associated sites.

The Folly, Settle 1679

PERIOD	EVENTS & *SITES ON THE ROUTE* (page references)
Mesolithic 10,000 BC – 4000 BC	The Middle Stone Age. Nomadic hunter-gatherers move over from the continent at the end of the last Ice Age. **Harpoon point, Victoria Cave** (47); **Microliths, Rombalds Moor** (25).
Neolithic 4000 BC – 2000 BC	The New Stone Age. People begin to settle, to clear woodland and to farm. Britain is now an island. **Cup-and-Ring marked rocks, Rombalds Moor** (25).
Bronze Age 2000 BC – 500 BC	Introduction of bronze and metal working. Farm settlements spread. **Twelve Apostles Stone Circle** (25); **Enclosure, Rough Haw** (38).
Iron Age 500 BC – 43 AD	Introduction of iron. The country is divided into Celtic tribal kingdoms; the largest is Brigantia. **Swastika Stone, Ilkley** (25); **Flasby Fell Sword** (37); **Hillfort, Ingleborough** (58).
Romano-British 43 AD – 410 AD	Romans occupy southern England and Wales. Eventually conquer Brigantes and occupy the north, AD 71. **Ilkley fort** (21); **Masongill hut circle settlement** (95).
Early Medieval 410 AD – 1066 AD	Dark Ages & Anglo-Scandinavian period. First Anglian settlers arrive around 450 followed by the Vikings in the late 700's. **Anglo-Saxon crosses, Addingham** (26) **& Ilkley** (21); **Viking-age farm settlement, Gauber, Ribblehead** (63).
Late Medieval 1066 AD- 1485 AD	The Norman Conquest & the Harrying of the North. Norman barons hand over much of the Dales to the monasteries. **Castlehaw, Sedbergh** (74); **Skipton** (30) **& Appleby Castles** (105); **St. Oswald's monastic house, Ravenstonedale** (91).
Tudor 1485 AD – 1602 AD	The Dissolution of the Monasteries leads to a period of relative prosperity for the Dales. **The Manor House, Ilkley** (21); **Moot Hall, Appleby** (104).
Stuart 1602 AD – 1714 AD	Civil War and revolution. The monarchy is overthrown and Oliver Cromwell takes power. **St Anne's Hospital and High Cross, Appleby** (105); **The Folly, Settle** (46).
Georgian & Victorian 1714 AD- 1900 AD	The Agricultural Revolution and the Industrial Age. **Salts Mill and Saltaire model village** (12); **White Wells spa bath house, Ilkley** (21); **Toll house and Turnpike road, Skipton** (30); **Ribblehead Viaduct & Settle-Carlisle railway** (106).

10

Wildlife of the Dales

Throughout the walk you will see a variety of wildlife depending on the time of year. Spring is the time to enjoy woodland flowers like **Bluebell**, **Primrose** and **Cowslip**. The grassland species such as **Early Purple Orchid** and **Bird's-eye Primrose** add speckles of colour on the pathside and migrant birds including the **Wheatear** and **Redstart** join the chorus of spring bird song. Butterflies such as the **Orange Tip** can be seen feeding on **Lady's Smock** – the food plant of their caterpillars.

As the days lengthen new flowers appear – the dominant orchid is the **Common Spotted** and you may be lucky to spot **Mountain Everlasting** on the slopes of Ingleborough. **Wild Thyme** and **Bird's-foot-trefoil** are common flowers seen in many sections of the walk throughout the summer. The hay meadows of Dentdale are splendid in June creating a swathe of colour and an insight into the interaction of humans and the landscape. Late summer flowers include the pale, delicate **Harebell** and the taller purple **Common Knapweed**.

The walk leads you through a series of habitats that are dictated by the underlying geology, and throughout the year you will enjoy the contrasts of woodland, river and fells. Much of the wildlife occurs throughout. During summer months **Skylarks** can be found from Rombalds Moor to Great Asby Scar and the distinctive bubbling call of the

Orange Tip butterfly
(*photo © www.northeastwildlife.co.uk*)

Heron
(*photo © www.northeastwildlife.co.uk*)

Curlew can be heard as it flies over its upland breeding sites. **Herons** can be seen fishing along the river stretches and **Kestrels** may be spotted hovering in search of prey. **Ravens** are confined to the higher ground as you reach the Dales and Howgills and can be distinguished from their more common cousins - the crows, rooks and jackdaws - by their size and the harsh *pruk-pruk* of their call.

Some of the wildlife is more elusive, but wonderful if you are lucky enough to spot it – **Red Squirrels** in the Eden Valley or the **Northern Brown Argus** butterfly on Ingleborough.

The wildlife pages give an indication of what you may see and will help the beginner identify some of the more common birds and plants. Photos have been allocated to the most appropriate section but the plants and animals may well be seen in other sections of the walk as well.

If you are keen to identify wildlife in more detail, including the trees, grasses and insects that are not mentioned in this companion, you need to consider carrying good field guides.

New Mill, Saltaire

SALTAIRE

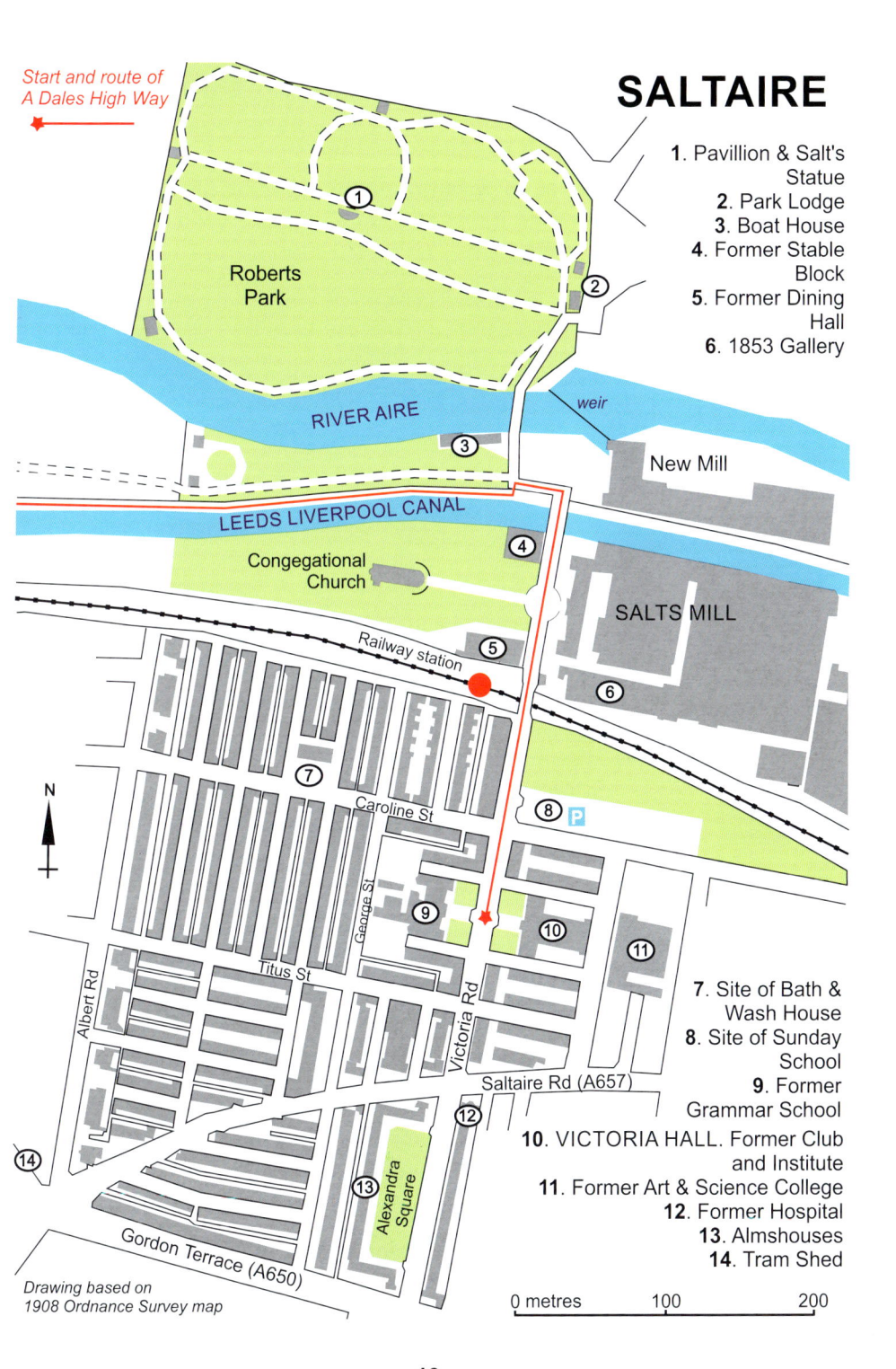

Start and route of A Dales High Way

1. Pavillion & Salt's Statue
2. Park Lodge
3. Boat House
4. Former Stable Block
5. Former Dining Hall
6. 1853 Gallery
7. Site of Bath & Wash House
8. Site of Sunday School
9. Former Grammar School
10. VICTORIA HALL. Former Club and Institute
11. Former Art & Science College
12. Former Hospital
13. Almshouses
14. Tram Shed

Roberts Park

RIVER AIRE

weir

New Mill

LEEDS LIVERPOOL CANAL

Congregational Church

Railway station

SALTS MILL

Caroline St

George St

Titus St

Albert Rd

Victoria Rd

Saltaire Rd (A657)

Alexandra Square

Gordon Terrace (A650)

Drawing based on 1908 Ordnance Survey map

0 metres 100 200

13

SALTAIRE - World Heritage Site

"Saltaire, West Yorkshire, is a complete and well-preserved industrial village of the second half of the 19th century. Its textile mills, public buildings and workers' housing are built in a harmonious style of high architectural standards and the urban plan survives intact, giving a vivid impression of Victorian philanthropic paternalism." - *UNESCO 2001.*

Daniel Salt moved his family to Bradford - "Wool City" - in 1822 and set up as a wool merchant. His son Titus became chief wool buyer to the family firm and was soon playing a leading role in introducing new materials to the spinning industry. By 1834 Titus had set up his own business and by 1843, with five mills in operation, he was one of Bradford's leading manufacturers.

However, Bradford at this time was a grim and dangerous place. Rapid industrialisation had seen the population mushroom from 16,000 to over 100,000 in just 40 years, swollen latterly by impoverished immigrants escaping the ravages of the Irish famine. Ten year old children laboured for 13 hours each day at factory machines, cajoled by the strap of the overlooker. Hundreds of mill chimneys blanketed the cramped town in a thick, choking smog. Life expectancy was just 20 years.

In 1848 German poet Georg Weerth wrote of Bradford: *"I wouldn't have felt any different if I had been taken straight to hell. Every other factory town in England is a paradise in comparison to this hole. ... if anyone wants to feel how a poor sinner is tormented in Purgatory, let him travel to Bradford."*

Chartists were beginning to organise against this new and brutal capitalism. By 1850 Titus Salt, now borough mayor, decided to move his business to a new greenfield site near Shipley.

The village

The site was perfect: plenty of land, adjoining the river, the canal and the railway line. Salt could bring the production of his five factories under one roof and maximise the benefits of mechanisation. First he built the mill. Completed in 1853, it was constructed of local stone in an Italianate style. The east-west alignment gave maximum natural light through its long, south facing façade and the huge room which filled the entire length of the sixth floor was regarded as the biggest room in the world at the time. Twelve hundred looms pumped out 17 miles of cloth each day.

Workers' cottages and boarding houses were built between Albert Terrace and Caroline Street the following year. The dining hall opposite the mill was also finished. The

Bradford as portrayed in the Illustrated London News, 1882

railway station opened in 1856 and a second housing phase, including the overlookers' cottages along George Street, was completed in 1858.

Statue of Titus Salt, Roberts Park

Over the next ten years a church and chapel, baths & wash-houses, schools, hospital and almshouses were all added. New Mill was finished in 1868 with Saltaire Park and the Club & Institute (now Victoria Hall) finally opening in 1871.

Conditions for workers at Saltaire had vastly improved but it came at a price. Almost all aspects of their daily lives were now controlled by Salt. They worked in his mill, rented his housing, shopped in his shops. Numerous regulations governed every daily activity - even hanging out washing was forbidden. Salt believed public houses fostered drunkenness and union militancy so there were none in the village. Instead the Club & Institute offered more wholesome activity - a library and reading room, chess room, smoking room, billards room, a lecture theatre, a concert hall and a gymnasium. But no alcohol. Titus Junior said it was there to **"supply the advantages of a public house, without its evils..."**

The Congregational Sunday school was the last building to open in 1876, the year Titus Salt died. Eleven years later his son, Titus Junior, who was now running the business, died suddenly aged just 44. Plans for a hotel, a covered market, an abattoir and further housing never materialised.

By now the vast profits enjoyed by the wool barons were in decline. In 1891, falling prices led Salt's major rival, Samuel Cunliffe Lister, to cut wages at his huge mill in Manningham. A strike led to a violent lock-out of 4,000 workers. The bitter five month dispute that followed saw troops deployed to quell rioting. In the end the workers were forced to capitulate, but within three years their aspiration for political representation saw the birth of the Independent Labour Party in Bradford.

By 1892 it was all over for Sir Titus Salt & Sons Ltd. The company went into liquidation.

Regeneration

Production continued in the old mill until 1986, when it was finally closed by its then owners, Illingworth Morris. The mill buildings stood empty, facing dereliction. Saltaire village was crumbling.

Enter Jonathan Silver - self-made clothing millionaire and visionary in search of a project. He found it in Salts Mill, which he bought at a knock down price. He brought art and retail into the old mill. A surprising mixture, but it worked. Manufacturing returned with high technology company PACE. New Mill was sold for redevelopment as residential and office space.

The reopening of the railway station in 1984 also had a huge impact. The mill cottages at the foot of the moors were very attractive to young commuters who were now only minutes away from Leeds and Bradford. New shops, bars and cafes appeared. Saltaire was soon booming again.

View along Albert Terrace, Saltaire (above), with the mill in the background.
Waymark at path junction on Burley Moor - eastern end of Rombalds Moor (below)

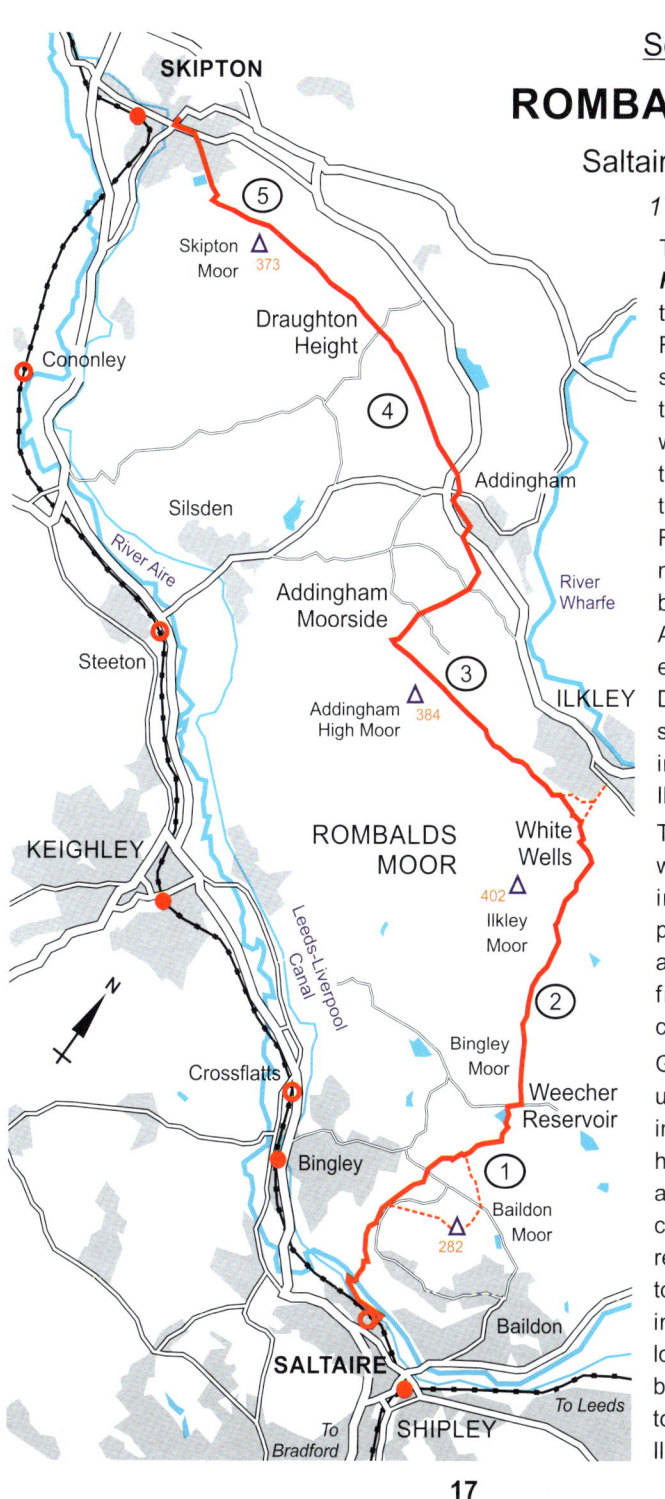

Section 1

ROMBALDS MOOR

Saltaire to Skipton

17.9 miles

The first section of **A Dales High Way** is dominated by the long whaleback of Rombalds Moor. Just a short way into your journey, the charm of Saltaire and its wooded valley gives way to the sweeping landscape of this exposed upland moor. Rombalds Moor is a long, narrow ridge, rising between Wharfedale and Airedale at the south eastern tip of the Yorkshire Dales. It is made up of several local moors including the celebrated Ilkley Moor.

There is much to interest walkers. Your route follows in the footsteps of our prehistoric ancestors and all along the way you can find examples of their culture.

Generally the going underfoot is good though inevitably on this typical heather moorland there are a couple of wet patches to cross. The highest point reached is 380 metres but a total ascent of 800 metres is involved. The section is long at just under 18 miles but there are opportunities to break your journey at Ilkley and Addingham.

17

1. Saltaire to Weecher Reservoir
[3.7 miles]

(1) **A Dales High Way** starts in front of Victoria Hall on Saltaire's Victoria Road.

Victoria Hall was formally called the Club and Institute. The Hall sits opposite the old Grammar School – now part of Shipley College – and the two buildings are guarded by four stone lions named War, Peace, Determination and Vigilance.

Walk down the road towards Salts Mill. Cross the railway and canal bridges then turn left to join the canal towpath westwards.

(2) After half a mile leave the towpath by the lock. Turn right on to Hirst Mill Crescent then right again along a track. Swing left to a footbridge to cross the river Aire.

(3) Walk straight ahead through the housing estate along the Bowland Avenue greenway to the bus turning circle. Cross the road to join the bridleway, marked **Dales Way Link**, heading to Trench Wood.

(4) At a junction turn left into the wood. *Certain indicator plants suggest that there has been continuous tree cover here for at least 400 years, which classifies this as an ancient woodland - one of the richest wildlife habitats in Britain.* Keep straight ahead along the main track, ignoring paths which drop down towards the reservoir or cut back up Shipley Glen.

(5) Eventually the track begins to rise gently up through the trees, narrowing to a rocky path before emerging onto Shipley Glen.

Looking back southwards Lister's Mill chimney dominates the skyline, sitting above Bradford - "Wool City" - in the bowl behind and to its left.

Continue north on the grassy strip between the rocks and the road. Where a wall on the opposite side of the road ends at a corner, footpath signs point straight ahead, left and up the hill to the right.

Here is an option to head straight up to the top of Hope Hill (see box opposite).

(6) Ignore the main path that drops away to the left through two bollards. Instead, as the road swings away to the right, continue straight ahead by a fingerpost on a rough track through the bracken passing an old quarry on your left. Head for the trees.

Here, at a small clearing, another track forks

Canal towpath, Saltaire

off to the right for a short way. A little way along this track sits a cup-marked stone, one of around 450 discovered on the moors, dating from the late Neolithic period, over 4,000 years ago.

(7) Cross another track and continue straight on to drop down to the trees. The path narrows and follows Glovershaw beck northwards until you eventually emerge via a stile onto Bingley Road. Cross over and head up the lane towards Golcar Farm.

(8) At Golcar Farm ignore the main footpath signed **Dales Way Link** which cuts around the right of the farmhouse. Also ignore a stile behind you that crosses into a field. Instead follow a fenced track up to your right leading to a waymarked stile by a gate.

(9) Cross the stile and follow the right field boundary towards another gate. Don't go through the gate, but turn left just before it, to continue with the fence still on your right. Cross a stile and follow the track bearing left to a gate at the foot of the golf course.

(10) Beyond the gate are tracks used for training racehorses. Follow the main track that leads straight away from the gate and swings right towards Birch Close Farm (many walkers use a parallel trod in the adjoining field).

(11) Go through a gate to pass left behind the houses, then follow the lane that leads to the left away from the farm. When a tarmac lane crosses you have a choice: either turn left to follow the lane past Weecher Reservoir and emerge onto Otley Road, or look for a stile immediately opposite. An indistinct path drops to cross the beck below, then rises to cross another stile. Swing right across a muddy field to a stile in the corner, then follow the wall on your right up to the main road directly opposite the wall stile onto the moor. This alternative route, though indistinct and muddy in places, avoids walking on the busy Otley Road.

OPTIONAL ROUTE: via Hope Hill

(*from end of 5*) Take the signposted track that heads straight up the hill through the bracken. Cross the Crook Farm Caravan Park access road and continue straight on rising sharply to the left of Dobrudden Caravan Park.

As you pass the caravan park, about half way along the wall on your right note the heavily cup and ring marked stone.

Continue past the front of the caravan park, straight ahead towards the top of Hope Hill and the trig point.

The top is covered by many old mine-shafts where poor quality coal was extracted from the 16th century onwards, with production peaking in the mid-19th century.

The panoramic views here are excellent. To the south, Bradford sits in its bowl, with Lister's chimney standing high above Manningham Mills in its foreground. Further to the west the wind turbines of Ovenden Moor crowd the horizon. East it is possible to see the remaining towers of the Aire Valley power stations in the far distance, including Drax. Further left the sharp edge of Otley Chevin dominates the Wharfe valley below. To the north this route will continue across open moorland.

Hope Hill is covered by many tracks. Head slightly east of north, along the track that drops from the brow of the hill, to cross the road from Dobrudden Park. Continue downhill to a car park at the edge of Baildon Golf Course. Follow the main track from the car park in a north westerly direction towards the brow of the hill ahead (Pennythorne Hill), passing the green (hole no. 6) on your right. At a fork take the left hand track to drop down to the edge of the fairway and follow this downhill to the gate at the bottom. Here rejoin the original route and continue on to Birch Close (para 10).

GEOLOGY: The rocks of the moor are of the Millstone Grit series, built with layers of shale and coarse sandstone known as gritstone.

The gritstone is fairly well drained but the shale creates an impervious layer, giving a typical peaty, boggy upland moor landscape. The layers of coarse sandy material and mud were deposited in a large river delta about 300 million years ago, washed down from the Scottish highlands. This sedimentary process can be clearly seen in the layered nature of the gritstone outcrops on Shipley Glen.

The gritstone has been quarried in the past to make millstones and also used in the construction of many local buildings.

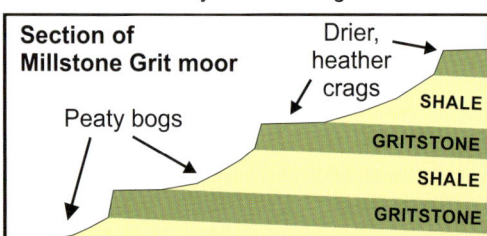

An abandoned millstone (right) lies in the valley below the gritstone outcrop on Shipley Glen (below)

Section of Millstone Grit moor

Peaty bogs
Drier, heather crags
SHALE
GRITSTONE
SHALE
GRITSTONE

Gritstone quarry on Addingham High Moor

White Wells - Victorian spa cottage on Ilkley Moor

ILKLEY is an attractive, prosperous town sitting beneath the escarpment of Ilkley Moor.

The Romans built a fort here in AD 79 as part of their occupation of the north of England. It was then known as **Olicana** (although there is some suggestion that the Roman name for Ilkley was actually *Verbeia*). Little of the fort remains now, although the site is obvious, marked by a raised grassy platform behind the Elizabethan Manor House. The remains of the western wall were uncovered by excavation in 1919 and can still be seen. The fort was finally abandoned around 400 AD.

Ilkley later grew as an Anglo-Saxon settlement and a striking set of stone crosses from this period can be seen inside All Saints Parish Church.

Ilkley became a fashionable Victorian spa town in the early 19th century with the construction of the vast Ben Rhydding Hydropathic Establishment a mile to the east. The coming of the railway in 1865 boosted the town's popularity.

The spa baths at **White Wells**, however, date back to 1703. Charles Darwin is believed to have "taken the waters" at White Wells when he visited Ilkley in 1859 whilst his book On the Origin of the Species was being published. Plunging into the cold waters of the bath house is still popular, particularly on New Years Day.

Bath house at White Wells

All that remains of the Roman fort - a wall and platform behind the Manor House

2. Weecher Reservoir to White Wells [*3.3 miles*]

(1) Emerge onto Otley Road from Weecher Reservoir and turn right. Care is needed here, as the traffic moves very fast. About 250 metres along the busy road cross a stile on the left. *This is an ancient packhorse route from Little London to Ilkley. This is Open Access land but dogs must kept on leads on the Right of Way path.* The way quickly climbs to a gate.

(2) The path now begins to swing in towards the wall on the right, to a double stile. *Beyond the stile is the meagre ruin of Horncliffe House and a boundary stone marking Horncliffe Well.* Do not cross these stiles, but continue up the hill, pulling away from the wall again.

(3) Soon, near Wicking Crag, the ground flattens and views of the moor ahead open out. *The view back to Weecher Reservoir and Hope Hill is splendid.*

(4) The path swings in again to meet the wall at a stile and gate. Once across, the ground becomes wet underfoot as the path continues in the same direction out onto the bleak moor.

(5) Eventually the track joins the main path from Eldwick at a waymark stone: "To Eldwick, Saltaire and Bingley. Ilkley 2 miles". This is also the **Dales Way Link** which was left at Golcar Farm. Continue north. The route is easy to follow all the way.

(6) Just before reaching the highest point of your journey over the moor, the **Twelve Apostles** stone circle beckons to the right. *Not as impressive as Stonehenge perhaps, but it is thought to have been built in the Bronze Age for much the same purpose – to celebrate the solstices.* A little further on is the ornate boundary stone called **Lanshaw Lad**. *The views here across Wharfedale are excellent. The white golfballs of Menwith Hill spy station are also visible on the distant horizon to the right.* The track here forks. Follow the right hand rough track dropping north.

Lanshaw Lad

(7) The way continues northwards, dropping to cross a wet patch, on old stone causeways and more recent flagstone paving.

(8) The path drops to cross Backstone Beck before rising again. *Down to the right, beyond the beck, is a plateau on which several Bronze Age settlements have been found. An area just visible from here known as* **The Enclosure** *was recently excavated and the base of an Iron Age roundhouse and enclosure walls dating from the Bronze Age have been partly reconstructed.*

(9) At the moor edge above Ilkley Crags, cross another track running along the ridge edge and begin to descend.

(10) Follow the main track as it drops steeply through the crags on a stone stairway.

(11) Eventually you reach White Wells cottage - *If the flag is flying, usually at weekends and holiday periods, then very welcome refreshments are being served and the old Victorian spa bath house is open for viewing.*

OPTIONAL ROUTE: From White Wells you can head straight down northwards along one of several paths to join the road into Ilkley, about half a mile away. Return up the same road, following it round to join the main route once again, just before Spicey Gill.

22

3. White Wells to Addingham Moorside [*3.5 miles*]

(1)   From White Wells, the main path swings down to the left heading west.

(2)   Just after passing a lovely little waterfall at Willy Hall's Spout, ignore the main path which drops straight down to the car park by the road. Look for another smaller track which cuts off to the left to follow the contour and join the Keighley Road just before Spicey Gill. Turn left along the road.

(3)   A little way on, a waymarked footpath cuts off the road to the right, crossing a footbridge to pass in front of the houses. The route is now easy, passing through a gate and following the moor edge all the way as it rises gently towards Addingham High Moor.

(4)   Just before the reservoir on your right, a clear green track forks off to the left, rising to run parallel to the moor edge to another gate. *Passing the reservoir, Addingham comes into view*.

Alternatively, continue alongside the wall. After crossing the footbridge above Heber's Ghyll, pass a wall stile. The wall now drops away to the right following a stream. Cross the stream and climb upwards towards the fenced rocky outcrop on the horizon. There are numerous tracks here, but continue up onto the ridge and join the main track to the fenced off Swastika Stone.

The Swastika Stone is unmissable, jutting above the escarpment edge in a fenced enclosure. The faint, Iron Age marking is on the large boulder, with a clear Victorian replica on a stone in front. The route here has probably been in use since the Bronze Age, linking the east and west coasts.

The way continues west clearly through several more stiles and gates.

Another fine example of cup and ring markings can be found further on at the Piper's Crag Stone, which juts out above the moor edge on the right, 30 metres beyond a second gate.

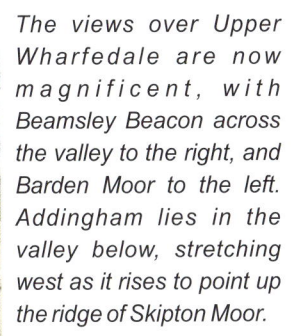

The views over Upper Wharfedale are now magnificent, with Beamsley Beacon across the valley to the right, and Barden Moor to the left. Addingham lies in the valley below, stretching west as it rises to point up the ridge of Skipton Moor.

(5)   Climbing gently towards Addingham High Moor top, the moor now opens into a heather covered plateau. A wall comes in diagonally from the left and beyond it the Aire Valley begins to come into view to the south, with Keighley prominent.

Roman family tombstone, Ilkley

(6)   At a waymarked cairn a path crosses from the left and drops through a gap to the right into a quarry. Follow this as it forks sharp right and descends below the cliffs as a rough, rocky track before gently swinging north to a stile.

(7)   The path now drops straight down across the field to a stile in the left corner. Cross this and follow the wall on the right, through a muddy section, down to a stile which leads out onto Moorside Lane at Addingham Moorside.

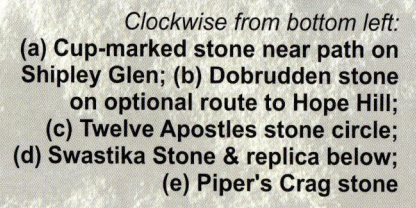

Clockwise from bottom left:
(a) Cup-marked stone near path on Shipley Glen; (b) Dobrudden stone on optional route to Hope Hill; (c) Twelve Apostles stone circle; (d) Swastika Stone & replica below; (e) Piper's Crag stone

PREHISTORIC ROCK ART ON ROMBALDS MOOR

Twenty thousand years ago, at the peak of the last Ice Age, Rombalds Moor was pretty much covered in ice. Huge glaciers had scoured the river valleys of Wharfedale and Airedale in a pincer movement, carving the moor between them before coming to an end just beyond Shipley. This was the southern tip of an ice sheet that stretched north across Scotland and Northern Europe.

It wasn't until the ice sheet receded - only around 14,000 years ago - that the first modern humans to set foot in the region finally arrived. They came from the Continent, walking across land that is now covered by the North Sea. These were the nomadic hunter-gatherers of the Mesolithic, or Middle Stone Age. They left behind thin flint slivers - microliths - that have been found on the moor, but little else.

Around 6,000 years ago their descendants began to settle on the moor. This marked the start of the Neolithic or New Stone Age. The moors then were very different from the way they are today. They were covered by a thin deciduous woodland. The climate was warmer and drier. The upland moor edges, sitting above the thickly forested and swampy valley bottoms, were the best places to live.

These Neolithic settlers began to clear the trees and to farm. They also created rock art, marking rocks with elaborate cup-and-ring designs. No-one really knows why, or what these strange markings really mean, but there are a lot of them. Over 450 examples have been catalogued on Rombalds Moor to date, with a similar number on surrounding moors.

Examples of prehistoric rock art can be found along the route of A Dales High Way. On Shipley Glen, just off to the right of the track (SE 1307 4009), is a rounded stone with four deep cup marks in an arc. On the optional route up the side of Hope Hill, standing half way along a wall beside Dobrudden Caravan Park (SE 1372 4009) is a stone with a very elaborate set of cup and ring markings. This stone originally lay flat on the ground nearby, but was moved and cemented into its current position by the Cartwright Hall Archaeological Group in 1954 for its own protection.

Just before the highest point on the moor is reached, walkers pass the stone circle known as the Twelve Apostles (SE 1260 4520). This is believed to date from the Bronze Age and is perhaps 3,500 years old.

Along the escarpment above Ilkley, the Swastika Stone is unmistakable in its fenced enclosure high above the Wharfe (SE 0960 4700). Dated much later than the cup and ring stones, this has greeted travellers since the Iron Age.

Further on at Addingham High Moor, jutting prominently from the moor edge, is the Piper's Crag Stone (SE 0849 4710), which carries 32 cups with ring and groove markings.

People have walked the track along the northern moor edge since the Bronze Age or earlier. Indeed, in 1946 local historian Eric. T. Cowling suggested it was part of a prehistoric trade route linking the east and west coasts. He called it Rombalds Way. It continues northwest from Addingham High Moor along the northern edge of Skipton Moor and through the Aire Gap to cross the Pennines.

This idea is now widely accepted. Tools made from flint brought from the Yorkshire Wolds in the east are found across the region. Neolithic axes made from volcanic tuff from the Lake District were carried in the opposite direction.

4. Addingham Moorside to Draughton Height [*4 miles*]

Addingham Moorside is a small, quiet farming hamlet with B&B accommodation.

(1) Cross straight over the road and follow the narrow lane opposite signed **Footpath for Addingham**.

(2) The lane follows a stream and after a short way it swings right to cross the stream. Just before this take a footpath to the left which runs through to a stile. Cross this and drop straight on down the field to pass a short stretch of wall on the left. Dogleg left and continue on to pass a line of trees on the left to a wall corner and a stile. Pass the caravan park on the left and follow the wall to cross two more stiles. The path now falls away to the right, funnelled down to a wall corner by a stream.

(3) Cross the beck at a footbridge and climb sharply up to the left, over a stile, to follow the wall up to the brow of the hill.

(4) Cross straight ahead towards a waymarked gate in a wall by a house. Through the gate the path turns right to follow the garden wall to a stile leading out onto a lane at Small Banks. Here turn left for a few metres to a stile on the right marked **Public footpath Addingham**. Cross the stile and head down the field following the wall on the right to cross two more stiles. The way now continues straight on across a field towards the trees to a wall stile. Beyond, descend a narrow enclosed paved track which drops to cross a footbridge before climbing the opposite bank to a stile.

Here there is an option to leave the main route and visit Addingham village. To do so head straight on and follow a faint track down the field, swinging gently left to meet a fence on the left at a corner. Go through a gate to drop and cross the very busy A65. Pass through a gate on the opposite side and along a narrow track leading down Stockinger Lane and into Addingham. From here follow the Main Street left as it climbs through the village. At a junction follow the road right onto Skipton Road, then left onto Moor Lane to rejoin the main route just before crossing the A65 again.

(5) The main route now turns left to follow the ridge. *On older Ordnance Survey maps this track is clearly marked* **The Street, ROMAN ROAD**. Through a gate pass to the left of Street Farm and continue beyond it along the ridge, through two more gates and past a mast on the right.

ADDINGHAM: Originally known as Long Addingham, this is an old Anglo-Saxon village. In 867 AD Archbishop Wulfhere of York hid in Addingham whilst fleeing the invading Danish Vikings. Syneon, an 11th century monk, tells how Wulfhere found refuge at *"Hatyngham in Hwerverdale, upon the bank of the River Hwerf between Otley and the Castle of Sciptun"*. An old stone cross dates from around this period and the shaft can be found in St Peter's Church (left).

Addingham grew substantially as a textile mill town during the Industrial Revolution. Here the first successful spinning mill was built at Low Mill in 1789 by John Cunliffe (grandfather of the more famous Bradford textile baron) and John Cockshott. It was the scene of a Luddite uprising in 1829.

Its long main street hosts several pubs and is well worth the optional diversion for a visit. Watch out for the ducks.

Moor Lane -"The Roman Road" - rises over Skipton Moor

(6) Watch for a partly concealed gate on the right, at a muddy spot just before the track opens out. Through this gate cross the very busy A65 taking great care. Through a gate on the opposite side, turn sharp left through another gate and along a fenced way, following the line of the main road on the left. Beyond another gate a narrow field begins to widen. Follow the track for a short while but then swing left to a stile in the corner.

(7) A gate beyond leads to a narrow track behind the houses. Pass through several gates before dropping to cross a stream.

(8) Swing right to follow the fence down the field, dropping steeply at the end through trees to cross a beck on stepping stones. Climb the opposite side, veering right to pass through a gate and along a track with the allotments on the left. Cross Addingham Main Street and go through a gate into playing fields. Swing left to climb diagonally across the field to a gate in the top right corner. Here turn right along the road to reach Moor Lane at a T-junction. Turn left and up to the main A65.

(9) Cross the busy main road with care, then continue straight on to follow the quiet Moor Lane as it climbs north west.

This continues along the alignment of **The Street** *and is known locally as* **The Roman Road**. *It is referred to as such in several official documents dating back to the early 19th century. It is widely believed to follow the line of the Roman Road from Ilkley to Elslack, just beyond Skipton, but there is, alas, no clear archaeological evidence to confirm this.*

The road continues for one mile, serving a scattering of farms, before the tarmac gives way to a faint track beyond the left of two gates, continuing straight on up.

(10) A wall comes up from the right to meet the track at a gate. Through the gate the path continues on the right side of the wall to another gate and then resumes on the left of the wall. *The view back to Chelker reservoir and beyond is lovely*. Continue on to meet the road at Draughton Height. Passing through the gate onto the road, note the milestone on the right.

Milestone, Draughton Height

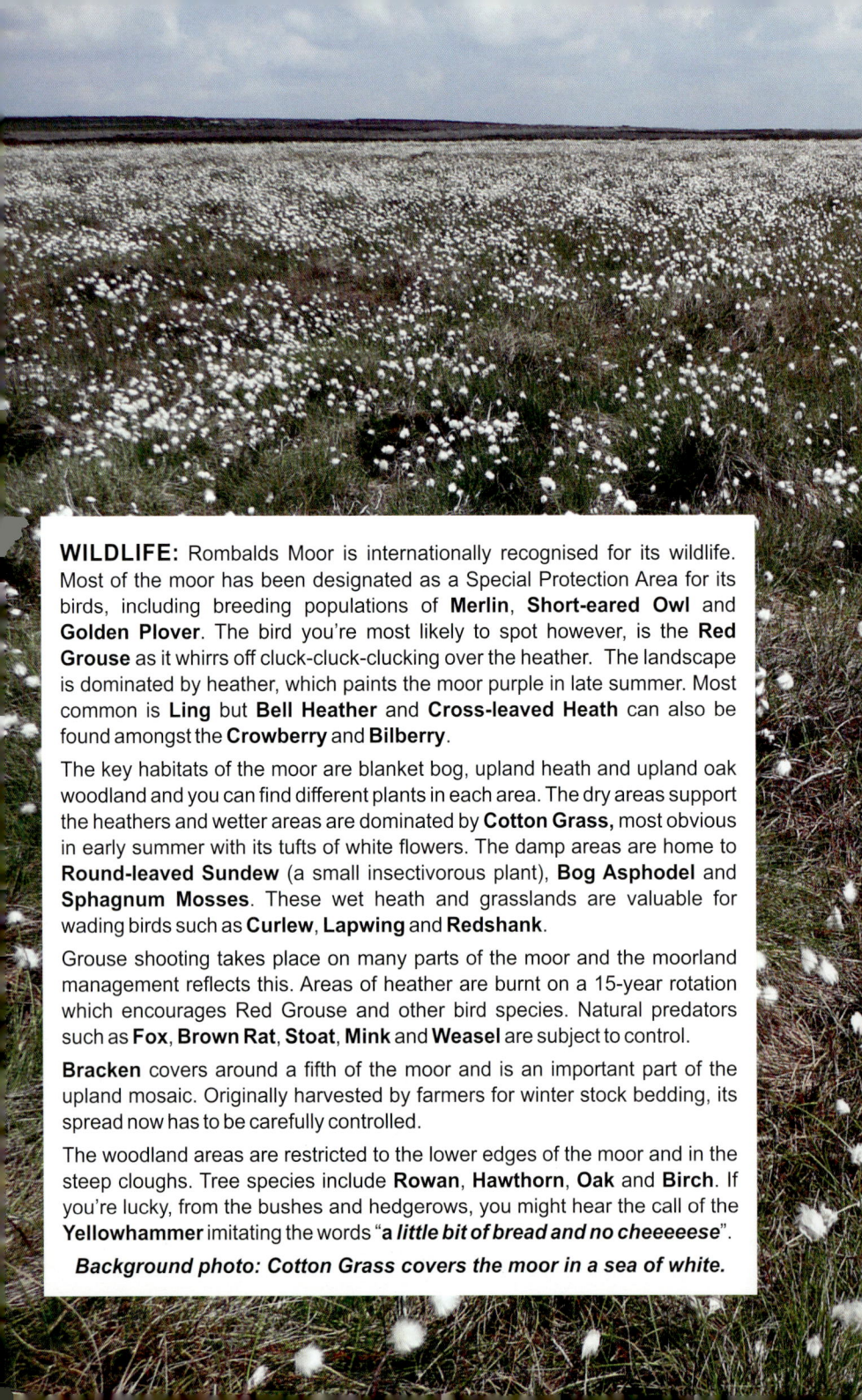

WILDLIFE: Rombalds Moor is internationally recognised for its wildlife. Most of the moor has been designated as a Special Protection Area for its birds, including breeding populations of **Merlin**, **Short-eared Owl** and **Golden Plover**. The bird you're most likely to spot however, is the **Red Grouse** as it whirrs off cluck-cluck-clucking over the heather. The landscape is dominated by heather, which paints the moor purple in late summer. Most common is **Ling** but **Bell Heather** and **Cross-leaved Heath** can also be found amongst the **Crowberry** and **Bilberry**.

The key habitats of the moor are blanket bog, upland heath and upland oak woodland and you can find different plants in each area. The dry areas support the heathers and wetter areas are dominated by **Cotton Grass,** most obvious in early summer with its tufts of white flowers. The damp areas are home to **Round-leaved Sundew** (a small insectivorous plant), **Bog Asphodel** and **Sphagnum Mosses**. These wet heath and grasslands are valuable for wading birds such as **Curlew**, **Lapwing** and **Redshank**.

Grouse shooting takes place on many parts of the moor and the moorland management reflects this. Areas of heather are burnt on a 15-year rotation which encourages Red Grouse and other bird species. Natural predators such as **Fox**, **Brown Rat**, **Stoat**, **Mink** and **Weasel** are subject to control.

Bracken covers around a fifth of the moor and is an important part of the upland mosaic. Originally harvested by farmers for winter stock bedding, its spread now has to be carefully controlled.

The woodland areas are restricted to the lower edges of the moor and in the steep cloughs. Tree species include **Rowan**, **Hawthorn**, **Oak** and **Birch**. If you're lucky, from the bushes and hedgerows, you might hear the call of the **Yellowhammer** imitating the words "*a little bit of bread and no cheeeeese*".

Background photo: Cotton Grass covers the moor in a sea of white.

(1) Ling (heather) (JP) *(2) Bilberry (JP)*
(3) Cross-leaved Heath (JP) *(4) Crowberry (JP)*

(5) Yellowhammer (N.E.W.) *(6) Curlew (N.E.W.)*
(7) Lapwing (N.E.W.) *(8) Red Grouse (N.E.W.)*

Toll House on Short Bank Road

5. Draughton Height to Skipton [*3.4 miles*]

(1)   Cross the road and go through a gate to join an easy, airy track as it leads on to pass Black Plantation on the right. *Barden Moor and Sharp Haw beyond come into view.*

From 1755 to 1803 this was the main Turnpike road used by coaches between Addingham to Skipton.

(2)   Beyond the plantation the track becomes muddy and rutted in places. *Skipton Moor rises to its summit on the left. To the right, stunning views open across to Barden Moor and beyond, to Sharp Haw and Rough Haw which await on the next section.*

(3)   Eventually the path begins a lovely gentle descent along a wooded track.

(4)   The path now passes a disused quarry, swinging sharply right to descend steeply, eventually joining Short Bank Road by the edge of Skipton. Follow the road straight on.

Watch out for the distinctive single storey Old Toll House on the right. Here you would have paid for the use of the route just taken. Eventually the road joins Newmarket Street, which leads left to join Skipton High Street.

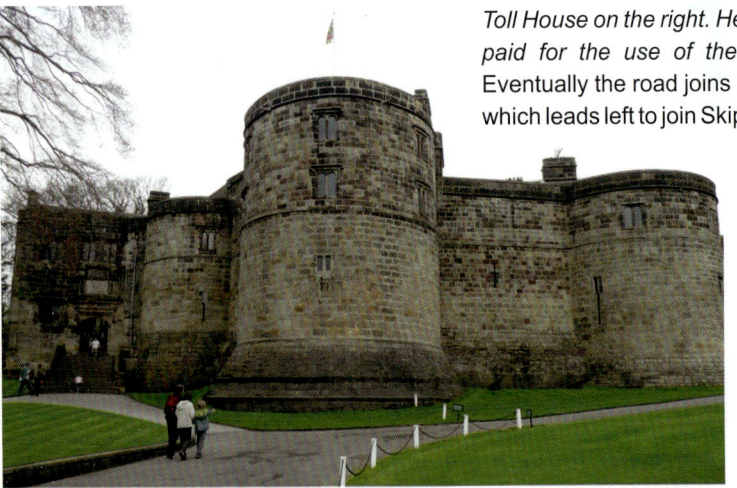

Skipton Castle (left), restored in 1659 by Lady Anne Clifford after the Civil War.

She planted a yew tree in the courtyard which is still growing (opposite page).

SKIPTON is the largest town you pass through on *A Dales High Way* and there's plenty to see and do in this lively, bustling market town. The High Street was winner of the 2009 *Great Street of the Year award* and prompted the judges to say **"Slowly, a lot of towns are becoming clone towns, but Skipton retains a very strong identity and character. It has a wonderful canal next to the high street, and it's such a beautiful setting."**

Skipton is situated in the Aire Gap between the limestone dales to the north, the gritstone moors to the south and the fertile Ribble valley to the west and is rightly proud of its title **The Gateway to the Dales**.

The name Skipton comes from the Saxon and means **sheep town**. It was originally a sheep farm and grew to be a trading centre for both livestock and wool. Robert de Romille, a Norman baron, built a wooden fort there soon after 1090 which was later replaced by the first Skipton Castle. In 1310 Skipton Castle passed to the Clifford family, and became their main residence for over 300 years. The castle was rebuilt by **Lady Anne Clifford** after the Civil War, and much of the present building dates from the 1650s. It is open to the public and is remarkably intact, being one of the best preserved medieval castles in England. If you have time it is worth a visit.

A market was granted its charter by King John in 1204 and continues to the present day. Visit Skipton on a Monday, Wednesday, Friday or Saturday and you'll find the cobbles along both sides of the High Street lined with stalls. The canal basin is in the centre of town and visitors can take boat trips on a traditional canal boat. Each year Skipton is the venue for the Skipton Waterways Festival, the largest annual meeting of canal boats in the north of England.

Malham Cove

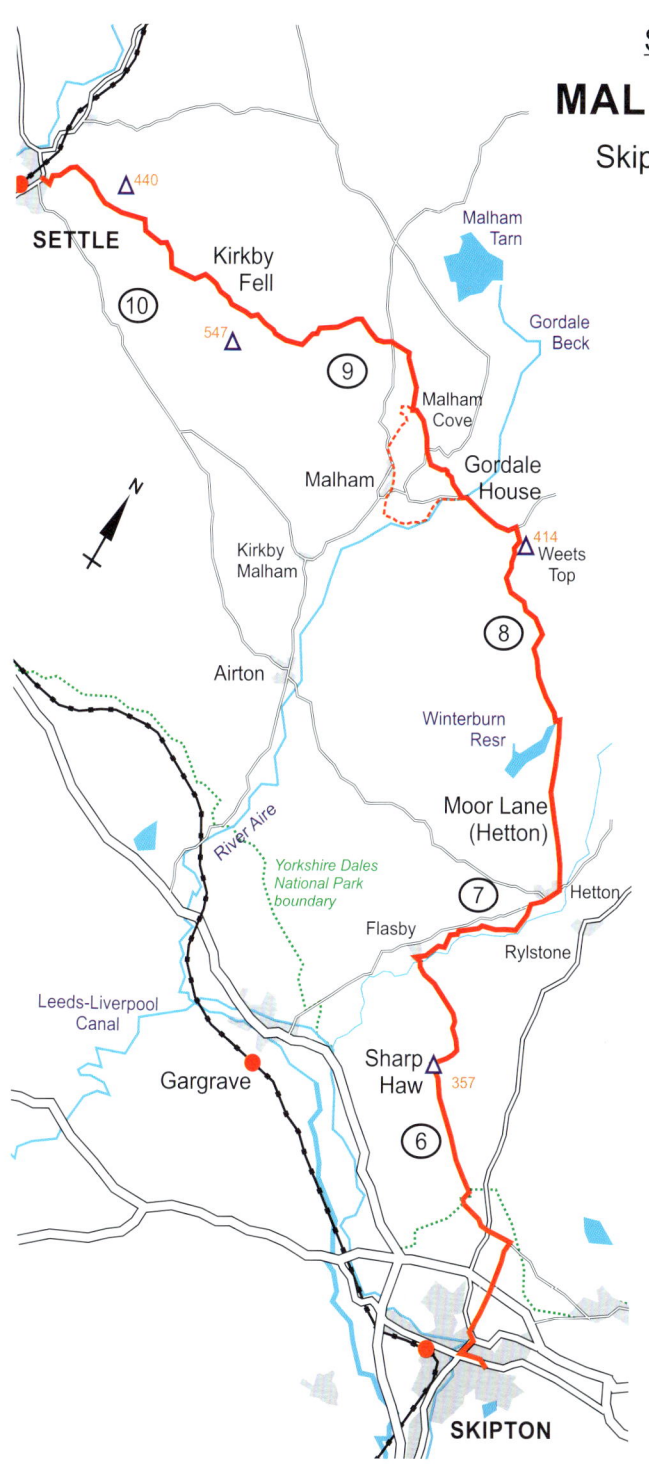

Section 2
MALHAMDALE
Skipton to Settle
18.7 miles

This section is a tale of two halves, marked by a dramatic and spectacular change in the landscape at Malhamdale. The first half covers more of the familiar moorland landscape. The climb up to the modest peak of Sharp Haw is rewarded with long panoramic views. From Flasby a delightful beckside ramble leads to Hetton, before the long climb to Weets Top reveals the stunning limestone country that awaits.

The route passes Gordale Scar, but a diversion here is a must as this awesome gorge is best appreciated close up. If Malham is the destination then a path by the lovely waterfall at Janet's Foss is recommended, otherwise continue to the top of Malham Cove and then on up to pass Kirkby Fell. The crags and scars of Attermire have a definite feel of the Wild West, before the charming Dales town of Settle is reached.

This section too is long, at 18.7 miles, but can be broken at Hetton or more likely at Malham.

6. Skipton to Sharp Haw *[3.5 miles]*

1. The first short stretch shares the route with the start of *Lady Anne's Way*. Walk up the High Street towards the church, taking the left fork at the top onto Grassington Road to cross the canal. Turn right up Chapel Hill and left at a footpath sign to cross a stile by a gate into the field.

A fine alternative route to the bypass follows a permissive path through Skipton Woods and Sougha Gill: join the canal side to head north just before Chapel Hill.

2. Follow the faint track steeply up Park Hill to a stile at the top. *An excellent view back over Skipton shows the town sitting below in the Aire Gap and Skipton Moor rising to the left. During the English Civil War the Parliamentary forces placed one of two cannon on the spot you're now standing, as they laid seige to Skipton Castle.* Cross the stile and continue northwards over the next field to the bypass. *The pointed peak of Sharp Haw is clear on the left.*

3. Cross a stile onto a lane. Opposite is another stile leading up to the busy bypass. Cross the road with care, go over a stile on the far side and up the hill to climb another stile onto the golf course.

An alternative safer route continues west along Short Lee Lane and up to the roundabout crossing, picking up a new footpath alongside Grassington Road to the Craven Heiffer.

4. The route is straight ahead, guided by pale green marker posts. Watch out for golfers! Cross a stile and go straight over another field, through a gate back onto the golf course and continue ahead along a track and out onto Brackenly Lane. Turn left up the lane to join Grassington Road at the top. *Just down the road on the left is the Craven Heifer Hotel.* Cross straight over, climbing a stile and heading up the field, swinging right to another stile by a powerline post. Climb over this and continue straight on westwards up past Tarn House Farm to a road. Follow the road ahead, zigzagging first right then left to reach a gate at the next right hand bend. *This point marks the Yorkshire Dales National Park boundary, which you are about to cross.*

5. Pass through the gate signed **Public Bridleway Flasby,** then up the farm lane and over two cattle grids until the moor opens out before you.

6. Where the wall on the left reaches a corner before heading away, head up a track forking off the lane to the right by a waymark.

7. Pass through a gate which marks the start of the Open Access area and continue rising, following the track straight towards the peak of Sharp Haw ahead.

Ignoring a right fork in the track, which bypasses the summit, continue up to cross a metal stile onto the top of Sharp Haw. A steel bench by the stile is a good place for a break. *Across from the trig point, north east, is the rounded peak of Rough Haw and beyond that the prominent cairn of the Rylstone War Memorial tops Barden Moor. To the left of that, in the distance, is Great Whernside. Ahead to the north lies the hamlet of Hetton,* the next destination.

Final push to the top of Sharp Haw

The Brigantes and the Roman Occupation

The transition from Iron Age Britain to Roman Britain also marks the transition from Prehistory to History – we now have written accounts, albeit from a Roman perspective.

Two thousand years ago Britain was divided into a number of Celtic kingdoms. The largest and most powerful of these was **Brigantia**, which covered much of the north.

This was also the time of the Roman invasion. Following earlier forays by Julius Caesar, the Emperor Claudius returned to occupy Britain in 43 AD. It was fairly easy for the Romans - the Britons were divided, with some Celtic chiefs making deals with the invaders whilst others chose to fight.

The **Brigantes** were ruled at the time by **Queen Cartimandua** and her husband **Venutius**. She chose to ally herself with the Romans. In 51 AD the famed Celtic warrior chief Caratacus, who had been fighting the Romans from the moment they landed, fled to Brigantia seeking refuge. Cartimandua had him bound in chains and handed over to the Romans - not a popular decision with her own people.

But the Romans didn't have it all their own way. In 61 AD the most famous of all the Celtic warrior chiefs – **Boudicca** – led an uprising that almost succeeded in driving the Romans from Britain. She attacked and destroyed the Roman settlement at Colchester, smashed the Roman 9th Legion, then destroyed London, before she was finally defeated.

Had Cartimandua and the Brigantes joined the rebellion, perhaps history might have been different. But they did not. By 69 AD Cartimandua had ended the increasingly acrimonious marriage to her husband Venutius, who now led an anti-Roman faction against her. Roman historian **Tacitus** says:

"Accordingly Venutius collected some auxiliaries, and, aided at the same time by a revolt of the Brigantes, brought Cartimandua into the utmost peril. She asked for some Roman troops, and our auxiliary infantry and cavalry, after fighting with various success, contrived to rescue the Queen from her peril. Venutius retained the kingdom, and we had the war on our hands."

Statue of Boudicca near Westminster Bridge in London

The Romans now had to raise an army against the Brigantes, led by Venutius. Sometime after 71 AD Roman governor Petillius Cerialis, who had led the ill-fated 9th legion against Boudicca, moved against Venutius:

"Petillius Cerialis at once struck terror into their hearts by attacking the state of the Brigantes which is said to be the most populous in the whole province. After a series of battles, some not un-costly, Petillius had operated, if not actually triumphed, over the major part of their territory." – (*Tacitus*).

Having defeated the Brigantes, the Romans now set about the military occupation of the north, building a string of forts such as the ones at Ilkley and Elslack near Skipton, linked by a network of roads.

However, they never really succeeded in subduing the Brigantes, and a low-level insurgency continued, breaking out into occasional major uprisings. It is worth noting that although there were extensive Roman civil settlements in the east, around York, only one Roman villa, at Gargrave, has been found in this region.

Flasby Beck (below).

(Right, clockwise) A young roe deer comes to graze beside Flasby Beck. Startled, it leaps a fence and heads back into the woods, stopping for a last glance before finally disappearing.

Looking back at Rough Haw and Sharp Haw from Moor Lane above Hetton

The Flasby Sword. In the 1840s a beautiful Iron Age sword and scabbard were found somewhere on Flasby Fell. The scabbard is made from beaten and cast copper alloy, lined with wood and decorated in a native Celtic style. The sword itself is made of iron. The handle and hilt are missing and there is some corrosion damage. Such a sword would have been the prized possession of a local Brigantian warrior of high status.

There is some mystery about its discovery. The sword is **"said to have been found with others"** and was apparently discovered on the surface **"on a moor near Flasby, in the parish of Gargrave, West Riding, at a spot adjacent to Roman remains, including a tesselated pavement"**. In 1846 it was exhibited at a York meeting of the Archaeological Institute by a Mr. Preston. In 1880 it was noted as being in the possession of Capt. Preston of Flasby Hall.

Two points are worth noting here: firstly the home of the Prestons - Flasby Hall - was built between 1843 and 1844; and secondly the only Roman villa to be discovered in the region was found at Kirk Sink, Gargrave, just two miles south of Flasby Hall. In 1962 Colonel J. Preston of Flasby Hall sent the sword to Sotheby's for sale and it was acquired by the Craven Museum at Skipton, where it is currently displayed.

It is similar to other northern swords of the first century AD, particularly one found at Melsonby, near the extensive Iron Age camp at Stanwick, believed to be the seat of the Brigantian queen Cartimandua.

Then in 2002 a remarkable Iron Age weapons cache was found buried in a field at South Cave, Humberside. It included 33 spearheads and five swords with beautifully decorated scabbards. It was buried with pieces of Roman pottery which allowed the burial to be fairly precisely dated to about 70 AD. This hoard is on display at the Treasure House, Beverley.

During the Iron Age this area lay beyond the eastern boundary of Brigantia and was occupied by the Parisi tribe. Although the Flasby sword is a much simpler design, the similarities with the South Cave swords are so striking that they may well have a common source.

By 71 AD the Roman army was moving north against the Brigantes. They crossed the river Humber near to South Cave. Although the Parisi are thought to have offered no resistance, the Romans are likely to have demanded they hand over all their weapons. Perhaps these high status swords were buried to prevent them falling into Roman hands. In any event, the person who hid them never returned to reclaim them.

Meanwhile the Romans turned west to attack the Brigantes and begin the military occupation of the north.

(photo © Craven Museum & Gallery)

7. Sharp Haw to Moor Lane (Hetton)
[4.2 miles]

1. From the trig point, a track runs north a little way before dropping right through a gap in the wall and heading down the field directly towards Rough Haw.

2. Through a gate a faint track leads straight ahead to climb Rough Haw, a pleasant enough diversion if time permits **(see box)**. Otherwise the main track forks slightly left to continue along a clear path.

Here a decision must be taken as to the best way to proceed, depending on conditions. With Rough Haw rising on the right and the woods beyond a wall down to the left, the general aim is to head straight ahead down through the bracken covered field, swinging left to reach a farm pasture. The main route follows the bridleway, clearly marked on OS maps. There are also alternatives to the right and left. Consider each in turn.

* *Main bridleway* – continue down the most obvious track a little way, heading towards the woods below, looking for marker posts. To the right of the track runs a parallel ditch, which marks the route of the bridleway. This soon veers off the more obvious track to the right, to head north through the middle of the bracken. It continues this way, following the line of the ditch and finally crossing a stream bed as it approaches a wall ahead. Swing left to follow the line of this wall as it drops north west, with the now deepening stream valley on your left. Cross a tributary stream which comes in from the right and eventually drop to a gate in the wall that crosses ahead and slopes down left to the stream by the woods below. Go through this gate and head diagonally down across the pasture to a gate

---

ROUGH HAW hosts a stone-built hilltop enclosure of unknown prehistoric date. There's not much to see, and what there is can best be glimpsed at the point you reach the edge of the first terrace, passing through a gap in the natural rocky outcrop. To your left the faint remains of the enclosure wall stretch away along the edge. This continues to the steep cliffs on the west and northern edges, where there are commanding views. The width of the rampart, where it exists, is fairly constant at 2.5m, with the outer face ranging in height from 0.8m to 1.8m. The top of the hill covers a huge area of about seven hectares (17 acres) with a sharp rise to the summit at the southern end.

The interior has been disturbed by post-medieval quarrying, so there are no ancient remains here. Much of the rampart stone was probably robbed out at this time as well. The site was first identified from aerial photographs in 1975 and tentatively described as a **hillfort**. Following field visits in 1996 and 1997 it was redescribed as a **prehistoric enclosure, probably Bronze Age.**

(Below) The embankment is seen on the left at the top of the track up Rough Haw.

in the far left corner that leads into an enclosed track.

This route is relatively straightforward in winter and spring. However, by high summer it is liable to become overgrown by thick bracken, to such an extent that even spotting it may be difficult and negotiating the bracken can be unpleasant.

Right alternative – just before the main track starts to descend, a faint track cuts off to the right to follow a contour along the western flank of Rough Haw, maintaining its height for a way and thus avoiding the worst of the bracken. Eventually it drops to join the main bridleway near the far wall.

Left alternative – this is the easiest and most popular track and the one you will use if you just follow your nose. The clear rough track drops to eventually join the wall on the left by the wooded area. The track continues down, following the wall on the left, with a stream to the right which eventually closes in to be crossed just before a gate where two walls meet. Go through this gate to follow the wall on the left through the pasture (though not strictly a right of way here) to another gate leading to the enclosed track. The problem with this much more obvious route is that it has become heavily eroded through use and so is best avoided if possible.

Whichever route you take, pass through the gate in the pasture onto the enclosed track.

Ahead go through two very muddy gates which straddle a crossing farm track. Beyond enter a delightful wooded greenway leading down to Flasby.

3. At the foot of the track ignore a footpath to **Rylstone** on the right and instead continue straight on to cross a bridge over the beck to another footpath sign on the right for **Hetton – 2 miles**. Pass through a gate and two small paddocks, through another gate and alongside the beck to a further gate.

4. Go through this and cross a stream. The track veers diagonally uphill on the left, to climb up along a field ridge with the beck well down to the right. Follow the ridge straight ahead as the beck recedes, before closing in again where a fence comes in from the left. Drop down towards the beck again. Crossing the fence through a gate, follow it on the right to a stile which leads over a farm track by a bridge, then over another stile to continue with the beck still down on the right.

5. Continue like this for some way, through three more stiles and a gate.

6. Eventually drop down close to the beck yet again at a footbridge leading to **Rylstone**. Ignore this and instead go through a gate straight ahead for **Hetton**. A narrow track now begins to swing away from the beck, rising to a stile. Cross another field and stile before heading finally to meet the road.

7. Follow the road right, into Hetton.

This quiet hamlet hosts the Angel Inn – famous for the quality of its food. Bed and breakfast is available, but at a price! However, a little further on at the road junction is the bus stop, with a fairly regular service into Skipton and Grassington.

*Nearby are the hamlets of Rylstone and Cracoe, which with Hetton mark the domain of the Rylstone & District Women's Institute. The story of their famous nude calendar was immortalised in the film **Calendar Girls** starring Helen Mirren and Julie Walters. To date the local WI has raised well over £3 million for charity. Rylstone also featured in Wordsworth's epic poem **The White Doe of Rylstone** and with luck you might spot a young deer coming down from the woods to drink from Flasby Beck.*

8. Passing through Hetton, take an enclosed track on the left, Moor Lane, signposted **Bridleway to Hetton Common**. This is an easy, gently rising green lane which leads up above Winterburn Reservoir.

WILDLIFE: The dramatic change in the landscape from peaty moorland to the limestone of Malhamdale brings new and distinctive habitats.

Step onto the limestone pavement above Malham Cove and look down into the deep cracks between the rocks. These grikes provide cool, humid, sheltered conditions which support woodland flowers such as **Wood Anemone**, **Bluebell**, **Dog's Mercury**, **Herb Robert** and **Wild Garlic**. Ferns like **Maidenhair Spleenwort** and **Hartstongue** can be easily spotted.

Malham Cove has been the home to **Peregrine Falcons** since 1993. They nest on the cliff face and feed on birds of all sizes. Feral pigeons are a favourite which they catch on the wing by making deadly accurate and high speed dives. Visit the cove between April and the end of July and watch these magnificent birds through telescopes set up at a viewing point run by the RSPB and Yorkshire Dales National Park Authority.

The wooded area at the foot of the cove is home to **Little Owl**, **Green Woodpecker** (which feed on colonies of **Meadow Ants**), **Great Spotted Woodpecker** and, in summer, **Redstart**. The rare **Jacob's-ladder** flowers on the lower slopes in June.

Throughout the walk, the **Skylark**, a species that has suffered dramatic decline in recent years, may be present. Although inconspicuous on the ground, it is easy to spot in its distinctive song flight. It has a small crest, which can be raised when excited or alarmed, and a white-sided tail, and is renowned for its vertical display flight. The **Meadow Pipit** is smaller than the Skylark and is also common on the upland moors.

Wheatear will accompany you in the spring and summer. The bird has a distinctive white rump visible as it flies, and it is thought that the name Wheatear originates from the Middle English meaning *white arse*.

(Below) The first of the 2008 Peregrine Falcon chicks at Malham Cove to fledge. (Photo © Neil Aldridge)

(1) *Maidenhair Spleenwort* (JP) **(2)** *Dog's Mercury (L) & Hartstongue (R)* (JP)
(3) *Jacob's-ladder* (JP) **(4)** *Autumn Gentian* (N.E.W.)

(5) *Skylark* (N.E.W.) **(6)** *Meadow Pipit* (N.E.W.)
(7) *Wheatear* (N.E.W.) **(8)** *Green Woodpecker* (N.E.W.)

8. Moor Lane (Hetton) to Gordale House *[3.8 miles]*

1. Pass through a gate as the lane levels out. The walls are now crumbling.

2. At the end of the walled lane a gate leads out on to the open moor. The track now forks, with Moor Lane continuing as a footpath to the right. Take the left fork signed **BW Malham**. As the track begins to drop, the reservoir down to the left comes into clear view.

3. The track swings leftwards down to the head of the reservoir and a footbridge across the beck. Leading up from the other side of the valley the ragged, deep sided line of Whetstone Gill is clear. Go over the bridge and through a gate to rise up with the stream well to the left beyond two walls.

4. The track is easy to follow up Hetton Common, passing several gates and rising all the way. *The view back over Flasby Fell and beyond to Skipton and Ilkley Moor is impressive. Pendle Hill begins to show to the west with Embsay Moor receding to the east. There is little here to disturb the quiet and solitude of this lonely moor.*

5. A slight drop leads to cross the waters of Ray Gill, passing through a gateway to continue up a recently restored path, dry and easy.

6. Swinging round to the left, above the wall, just below the top of Hetton Common Head, the view opens out to the west, with Kirkby Fell dominating the scene. Ahead lies Weets Top, marked by the surviving upright of an old cross, and a trig point over to the right.

The panoramic views here are magnificent. Ahead the limestone crags stand in sharp contrast to the gritstone moorland just crossed. The deep chasm of Gordale Scar lies below, and beyond rises Kirkby Fell. To the right lies Fountains Fell, with Ingleborough peeking through the gap. To the northeast Great Whernside dominates the view, leading round to Simon's Seat and then on to Barden Moor. To the west stands solitary Pendle Hill. Weets Top is a confluence for several paths and a meeting point for walkers, runners and cyclists.

7. From Weets Top a walled track runs down to join Hawthorne Lane, which descends steeply left to Gordale House. *The opening vista of the limestone crags to the right along the way is exhilarating.*

Just past Gordale House, a path runs off to the right into Gordale Scar, and unless time is pressing or legs are too tired for detours, the wondrous sight of the the scar's inner chasm beckons. One of the wonders of the Yorkshire Dales, it is not to be missed!

MALHAM

42

9. Gordale House to Kirkby Fell [3.8 miles]

1. The lane leads down to Gordale Bridge, where, with luck and good timing, the tea van will be parked and open for business.

As you descend the lane to Gordale House, you are following the line of the Mid Craven Fault. This fault marks the boundary between the bright, velvety green limestone terrain on the right and the rougher, darker moorland terrain on the left. The difference is quite striking. The fault continues onwards in a line passing just above Malham village to cross between Kirkby Fell and Grizedales, then down along the line of Stockdale Beck. Apart from a brief detour around the back of Malham Cove to Langscar, the route of this walk follows the line all the way to Settle.

The route continues from the bridge through a gate on the right leading to Malham Cove.

An alternative route into Malham village can be found a little further along the road, through a gate on the left marked **Janet's Foss**. *This is a delightful, easy walk through woodland following Gordale Beck. Janet's Foss is the waterfall at the start. A stopover at Malham is highly recommended! The main route can be rejoined from the village by walking up the Cove Road and turning right through a gate for Malham Cove. Climb the stone stairwell to the left of the cove and cross the limestone pavement on the top.*

2. The path climbs, following the wall on the right, to a gate. Continue straight over to another gate, then with the wall to the left follow the foot of the crags around to meet a road heading down to Malham. *If you're walking in August and September look out for the* **Autumn Gentian** *in the rocky areas with its clusters of purple flowers. It's also called* **Fellwort**. *Looking back up the valley the remaining signs of medieval farming terraces, or lynchets, give a corrugated look to the fields and are evident leading up the valley.* Cross the road and stile to continue along an easy green track, keeping left at a fork, leading to the top of Malham Cove.

3. At the top of the cove, turn right and follow the **Pennine Way** to a stile on into the Dry Valley. The path becomes increasingly rocky and if wet, can be very slippery.

4. Eventually a steep climb up a rocky stairway leads to a stile at the top, where tracks run off ahead and back to the right (the Pennine Way). Climb the stile just ahead on the left, before a wall corner, to follow a broad green track with a wall to the right up to the road at Langscar Gate.

5. Cross the road by the cattle grid to continue directly ahead, through a gate signed **Byway, Cow Close Langcliffe**. Continue up a stony track, which swings first left, away from the wall on the right, before swinging in again to a gateway at the top right corner of the field.

6. Beyond this the stony track continues onwards, but a broad green track cuts off to the left signed **PBW** to **Stockdale Lane**. Follow this track up, passing through three gateways to the foot of Grizedales.

Looking back Malham Tarn lies in full view. Also Pen-y-ghent eventually peeks through between Grizedales and Fountains Fell. Ahead on the wall to the left is the restored base of Nappa Cross which once stood further on by Nappa Gate. There are excellent views back to Weets Top from here.

7. At Nappa Gate a **PBW** post points up to the right to **Stockdale Lane**. Follow this route, passing between Kirkby Fell on the left and the top of Grizedales on the right. *If time permits, a detour to the top of Kirkby Fell, via a gate at the end of the wall, gives rewarding views down Malhamdale and serves to emphasise the difference underfoot of the terrain on either side of the Mid Craven Fault.*

GEOLOGY: Beyond Weets Top the landscape changes suddenly from peaty moorland to velvety limestone. The sharp change is marked by the **Mid Craven Fault**, an ancient fracture of the earth's surface caused by earthquakes. The fault runs east-west as far as Settle. North of the fault the land has risen, to the south it has sunk.

The fault developed during the Carboniferous Period when the sediments that make up the local bedrocks were still being deposited. To the south the limestone layers are now deep below ground level, covered in shale and topped with Millstone Grit. To the north the limestone scars rise up along the fault edge.

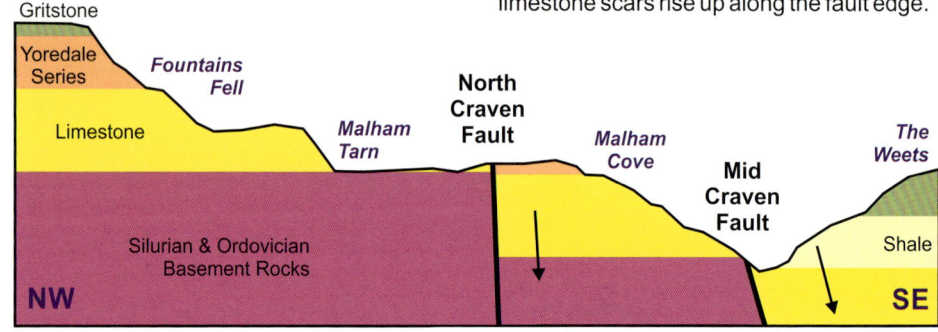

The route of *A Dales High Way* follows the fault, down Gordale Lane from Weets Top. As you walk down, left is moorland, right is limestone. The contrast is remarkable. After a brief diversion onto limestone country above the cove, the route rejoins the line of the fault at Nappa Gate and follows it more or less down to Settle.

Looking east from Malham Rakes. Gordale Scar is beyond the ridge on the left. Weets Top is on the right. The Mid Craven Fault runs along the line of Gordale Lane.

During the Ice Age, ice sheets scoured the tops of the limestone pavements. When the ice finally melted, great torrents of melt water cut the deep ravine of **Gordale Scar** *(top)*, and also poured down the now Dry Valley of Watlows to cascade over the edge of Malham Cove in a tremendous waterfall.

Rain that has absorbed atmospheric carbon dioxide becomes weakly acidic and when it falls on the limestone pavements, over time it eats into cracks. Eventually deep fissures, called **grikes**, are formed between the raised blocks, called **clints**. This produces the distinctive, denture-like limestone terracing known as karst *(bottom)*.

Gordale Scar

Limestone pavement above Malham Cove

10. Kirkby Fell to Settle *[3.4 miles]*

1. Over the brow, the track begins to drop down above Stockdale Farm, becoming increasingly rocky. The track squeezes in between the steep crags to the right and a wall on the left. *Rye Loaf Hill is prominent on the left.*

2. Passing the farm, a gate by the farm entrance leads out onto a tarmac lane – Stockdale Lane.

3. Where the lane takes a fairly sharp left bend, a gate to the right and behind leads back into a field and along a track marked **FP Settle**.

Ahead to the right the awesome crags of Attermire Scar present themselves, with the Wild West peaks of Warrendale Knotts beyond. The contrast between the terrain on the right and the peaty moorland on the left couldn't be greater and marks the line of the Mid Craven Fault.

The track curves gently through several fields, descending to the foot of Attermire Scar. *Another track leads up beside the Scar, heading north towards a number of well-known caves, including Victoria and Jubilee Caves, which are well worth exploring if time and energy permit. Another faint track cuts back up the face of the escarpment, leading to a tricky scramble up to Attermire Cave. Ahead the track rises once more passing Warrendale Knotts on the right to overlook Settle below.*

Long views westwards open out, dominated by the high peak of Ingleborough ahead. In the far distance, you can just make out the southern Lakeland Fells.

4. The track begins to drop steeply down towards Settle, swinging left to cross a broken wall before joining a walled track down to the outskirts at Constitution Hill. It is a short walk down into the town centre.

SETTLE is a delightful Dales market town sitting on the banks of the river Ribble, below the towering rocky outcrop of **Castleberg**. This limestone edifice is a magnet to climbers, but a series of paths, first laid out in the eighteenth century, provides an easy ascent for most people. The views from the top are outstanding.

Settle is the southern point of the famous Settle-Carlisle Railway, although the line itself extends to Leeds and Bradford.

The Folly is a Grade 1 listed building in the centre of town which dates from 1679 and houses the Museum of North Craven Life.

Settle is a good place to stay with plenty of accommodation, shops and food. There's a lively street market in the square every Tuesday.

Climbers tackle the rock of Castleberg

THE CAVES OF ATTERMIRE

On a fine May afternoon in 1837, a Langcliffe man called Michael Horner was out rabbiting in the hills above Settle with two companions and their terriers. One of the dogs disappeared into a "foxhole",

Climbers above Attermire Cave

reappearing some time later from another hole higher up. Horner climbed up, dragged away a large stone and slid inside. He found himself in a wide, low cave. Horner later told his boss Joseph Jackson, a plumber, about his discovery. Three weeks later on 20th June 1837, the day King William IV died and his niece Victoria became queen of England, Jackson climbed into the cave.

Exploring the low chamber, Jackson found a small opening in the north wall. Moving a pile of rocks he crawled into another, much higher, chamber, and in it he found a treasure of Roman artefacts. They include bronze brooches, bracelets, rings, earrings, buckles, bone spoons, glass and amber beads and shards of pottery. Over 100 coins minted between 83 BC and 346 AD have been recovered. How so much ancient material found its way into the cave remains a mystery, but ritual deposition over a long period is suspected.

Between 1870 and 1877 Victoria Cave was subject to a prolonged excavation and the cave entrance was greatly extended. Beneath the level of the Roman finds, layers of clay revealed the bones of numerous animals. At the higher levels were the remains of bear, lynx, fox, badger, horse and red deer. At the lowest levels were those of hippopotamus, straight-tusked elephant, rhinoceros, brown bear, spotted hyena, giant deer, red deer, bison and a lion. These lower finds have since been dated to a period 120,000 years ago, a time before the last Ice Age.

Outside the cave, beneath a rocky overhang, the team discovered a bone harpoon point. This has since been radiocarbon dated and is almost 11,000 years old. It represents the first major piece of evidence of human activity in the region.

Victoria Cave is just one of over 40 caves in the Dales in which archaeological remains have been discovered, though undoubtedly the most important. Others nearby include Jubilee Cave, Albert Cave and Attermire Cave. Cave archaeology is now an important area of research.

11,000 year-old barbed harpoon point, made from deer antler. Victoria Cave.

On top of Malham Cove (above).   The Dry Valley (below).   Attermire Scar (bottom)

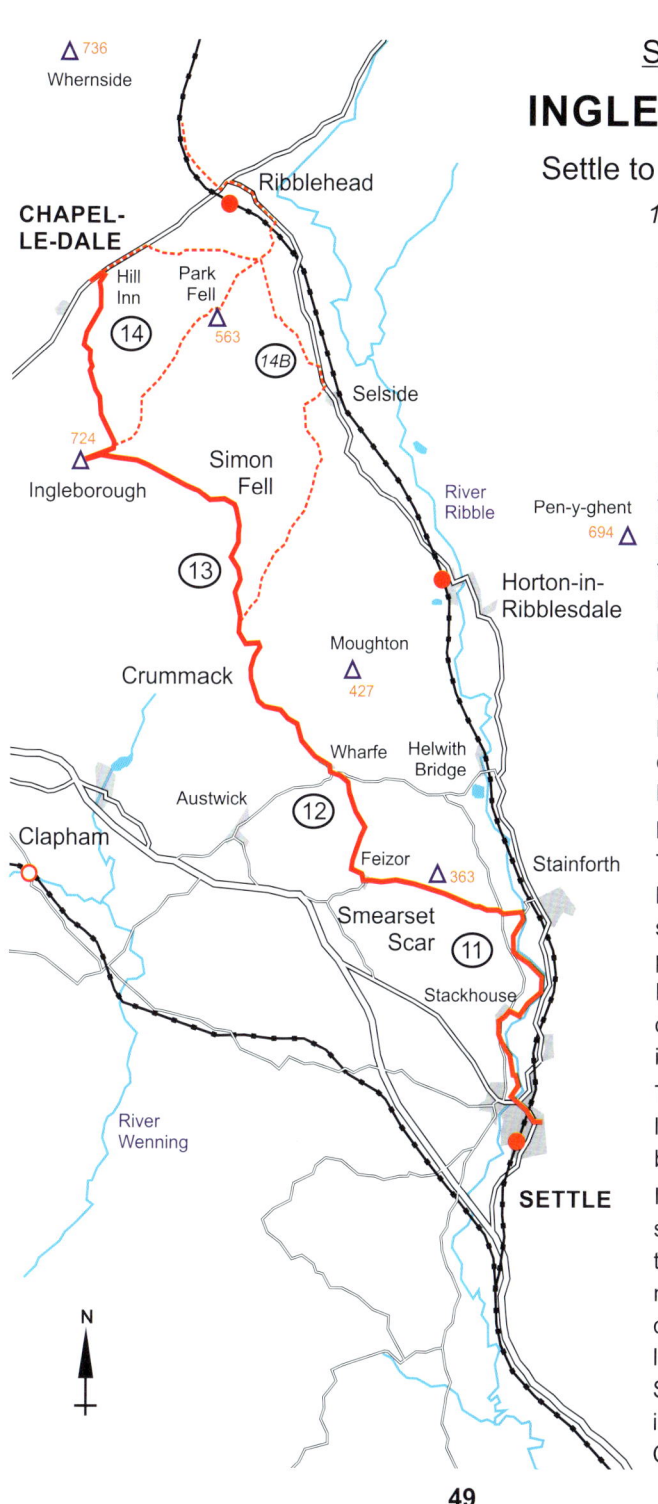

Section 3
INGLEBOROUGH
Settle to Chapel-le-Dale
14.2 miles

The final challenge of this section is the climb to the summit of the mighty Ingleborough, favourite of Yorkshire's Three Peaks.

The section begins with a lovely riverside walk along the banks of the Ribble to Stainforth Force. A trek over the limestone plateau beside Smearset Scar leads down into the quiet and secluded valley of Crummack Dale. A stop beside the clapper bridge over the bubbling Austwick Beck marks the halfway point.

The climb out at the valley head brings you onto the spectacular limestone pavements beneath Ingleborough and the start of the final ascent on the iconic Hollow Mountain.

There are alternative low level routes here should bad weather close in.

It is a long easy climb to the summit. After lingering on the broad, enigmatic mountain top, a sharp descent leads you onto the lovely limestone terrace of Souther Scales and down into the tiny hamlet of Chapel-le-Dale.

11. Settle to Smearset Scar *[4.1 miles]*

1.   From Settle town centre, turn north down the main road (Church Street) to pass under the railway bridge and cross the river Ribble heading towards Giggleswick. Once across the bridge, turn right along a track between sports fields. By the river turn left and follow the river to a stile.

2.   Go over the stile and cross the middle of the field, gently rising, to cross three more stiles; you are now high above the river on your right.

3.   The path now crosses a field to meet Stainforth Lane. Turn right and follow the quiet lane past Stackhouse. A gate beside a house on the right leads into a walled track signposted **Ribble Way, Stainforth**. Follow the track down to the weir.

4.   By the weir turn left to cross a stile leading along the riverside to Stainforth Bridge.

5.   The path now follows the Ribble all the way to Stainforth Bridge. This is a delightful walk, sometimes climbing up away from the river before dropping to rejoin it.

6.   Eventually pass the campsite on the left, through a gate to come out on the crags overlooking the waterfalls at Stainforth Force. This is a popular spot and in autumn people gather to watch the salmon as they leap up the falls against seemingly impossible odds to climb the river to spawn. The route continues to a stile beside the bridge to follow the lane up to the left, passing Little Stainforth and crossing Stainforth Lane to pass through a gate onto a farm track.

7.   A stile at the top of the track on the right is waymarked **Feizor**. Once across the stile the farm track veers right before turning west once more as it climbs, quickly becoming a broad green path rising to a stile beside a gate in a wall ahead.

There are fine views back to Pen-y-ghent and Fountains Fell. At the brow of the hill, with Smearset Scar ahead to the right, on the horizon ahead to the left stands the Celtic Wall. It looks like a short stretch of impressive dry stone walling. Once thought to date from the Iron Age and believed to mark an ancient burial mound, it is more probably of Medieval origin.

Stainforth Force, and an acrobatic Salmon leaps the fall (inset).

12. Smearset Scar to Crummack
[3.7 miles]

1. Passing Smearset Scar on the right, the broad green track begins to drop towards the hamlet of Feizor, crossing three more stiles on the way. *There are fine views ahead of the Forest of Bowland Fells (although without a trace of forest).* Finally crossing into the field above Scar Close Farm, the faint track drops to the bottom left corner along a tree line above a stream bed.

2. Several stiles and gates lead out onto Kiln Hill Lane in Feizor. *With luck, Elaine's farmhouse cafe opposite is serving tea and refreshments.* Finally head right, up the road.

3. The road swings left by a row of cottages to a gate, marked **PBW**. Beyond, the rough lane climbs and swings right, passing between crags on the right and woods on the left. After passing Wharfe Woods on the left the view ahead opens out, with Moughton Scar and Pen-y-ghent beyond.

4. Just a little way down the track towards Higher Bark House Farm, cross a stile on the left. *Ahead the tiny hamlet of Wharfe nestles at the foot of Crummack Dale with Ingleborough rising directly behind to dominate the view.* The path drops across fields by the woods on the left, via two gateways and three stiles, to a lane crossing its way.

5. Look for a stile across the lane where a stream appears under the wall. Across a field and another stile, a small footbridge leads across a stream by a delightful little waterfall on the left.

6. A further stile leads to a long field, where the faint path veers to the left, eventually crossing another stream on a small footbridge before joining the road ahead.

7. Follow the road down to the left a little way, to a private lane on the right marked **Bridleway to Crummack**. The lane leads up to a row of cottages, swinging left to cross in front of them.

8. The track continues above and behind the tiny hamlet of Wharfe, continuing along a walled track.

The path from Wharfe

9. The bridleway now follows an easy walled way right to Crummack.

10. Ingleborough disappears from view again. Just beyond a fork in the track you cross Austwick Beck by a clapper bridge. This is a popular picnic spot. Wash Dub field is so named because here the beck was regularly blocked to give a pool for sheep dipping. A little further on, the track joins Crummack Lane, where you turn right and follow the road up to Crummack Farm.

GEOLOGY: The oldest sedimentary rocks in the region are exposed in the valley bottom of Crummack Dale. These are mudstones, slates and sandstones laid down over 400 million years ago, in the Silurian and Ordovician Periods. These ancient rocks are best seen beyond Wharfe, exposed just to the north of Wash Dub field and Austwick Beck. The particular Silurian sandstone here is called **greywacke**. The dry stone walls bounding the route here are constructed from it.

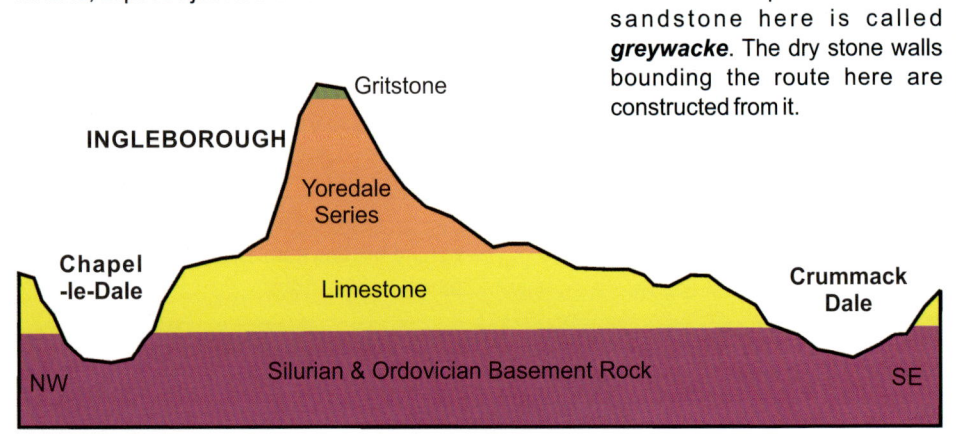

These **basement rocks** were originally laid down in horizontal beds, but earth movements have since folded and tilted them (*shown on the bottom half of the photo, left*). Later, during the Carboniferous Period, horizontal limestone beds were deposited on top. These formations can be seen on the eastern valley slopes north of Studrigg Scar. The clear line separating the two layers - an **unconformity** - marks a period of 60 million years when the land was above sea level and no new sediments were laid down.

Norber Erratics.

During the last Ice Age a glacier pushed over Moughton and down Crummack Dale, breaking chunks off these ancient rocks and carrying them down the dale and up onto the south western flanks of the valley. When the ice melted, the boulders were dumped. Many were scattered on top of the limestone terraces of Norber. Weakly acidic rain has since worn down the limestone surface, except where it was covered by the boulders, leaving some perched on precarious limestone pedestals *(right)*.

The area around Ingleborough is potholing country. Deep shafts and long passageways have been eaten into the Great Scar Limestone by slightly acidic rainwater, running from the impervious Yoredale rocks above. Many potholes can be found around the 400 metre mark where the two rock strata meet.

One of the largest underground caverns in the country is here, at **Gaping Gill**, which lies off-route below Little Ingleborough. The waters of Fell Beck plunge over 100 metres into the cathedral-like main chamber, which leads into one of the longest and most complex cave systems in the country. Best reached from Clapham, each year members of the public get the opportunity to explore the cave when Bradford Pothole Club organise a winch meeting over the Whitsun holiday period. Craven Pothole Club organise a similar event around the August Bank Holiday. For a modest fee you get lowered on a cabled chair into the floodlit main chamber *(above)*.

For the more faint hearted, there's the fascinating Ingleborough Show Cave on the route up to Gaping Gill. The White Scar Show Cave in Chapel-le-Dale can be reached by car.

13. Crummack to Simon Fell
[2.4 miles]

The route followed here crosses open ground where there are many tracks, so care is needed.

1. Go through two gates and head on, passing the farm on your right. A sign for Sulber points upwards to the left before the wall corner. Go up along a broad green track.

2. The track rises fairly steeply, swinging above a small hill on the left. The path forks, with a track running up to the right parallel with the wall line. Stick with the main track swinging left away from the wall.

3. The track climbs, veering right as it rises to head north. Ignore smaller tracks heading off either side and keep with the main broad track. Eventually the ascent eases and Ingleborough comes into view. At the brow of the hill ahead there is a confluence of tracks. Here take the main path crossing to the right, the **Pennine Bridleway (PBW)** heading just east of north. This is the ancient drove road from Clapham - **Long Lane** - which runs to Selside and beyond.

4. With Ingleborough to the left, follow this path for about 200 metres, ignoring a faint track off to the left which heads between two rocky outcrops into a U-shaped clearing. Just beyond the second rocky outcrop where a small **PBW** marker stands to the left of the path, a major track forks off to the left, heading up towards Simon Fell. This is an easy, clear path, about a metre and a half wide, a former Turbary (peat-cutters) Road.

*If the weather is too bad to attempt the peak, the alternative here is to continue straight on along the track (PBW) towards Selside, following an easy low-level route round to Ribblehead or further beneath Park Fell to join the main road into Chapel-le-Dale (see box **Alternative bad weather route**).*

5. The track heads roughly north, climbing above magnificent limestone pavements with Pen-y-ghent impressive in the distance. Rather disconcertingly you seem to be heading past Ingleborough which is away to the left. Press on until you meet a wall coming in from the left. This leads on to join the **Three Peaks** track climbing from the right alongside a wall.

6. Turn left to follow the main Three Peaks route up. The track climbs through potholing country, through a gate by a stream, to meet the ruin of an old shooting hut. *To the left is a large, rough wilderness called* **The Allotment** *which hides a number of deep potholes.*

7. The path continues alongside the wall on the right to cross the southern flank of Simon Fell on the way to the summit of Ingleborough.

Closing on Ingleborough along the southern flank of Simon Fell.

Alternative bad weather route to Ribblehead and Hill Inn (Chapel-le-Dale)

As you climb above Crummack Dale, if the weather proves too bad to tackle Ingleborough itself, then this alternative low-level route is a fascinating way in its own right.

Continue along the broad green track (Pennine Bridleway) straight on. *This is the old drove road from Clapham to Selside and beyond. Crummack Dale Head comes into view on the right, rising to the limestone terraces of Thieves Moss, with Pen-y-ghent magnificent above.*

Beyond Sulber Gate you reach a crossroads. Continue straight on the Pennine Bridleway for **B6479** (Selside). *If you need a quicker escape route, follow the Three Peaks track, right, down to Horton-in-Ribblesdale.*

This is a fine walk, with Simon and Park Fells on the left, Pen-y-ghent across to the right, and Cam Fell ahead. Through a gate go straight on, taking the right track at a fork, to drop to another gate. Through this turn left and cross the field, go over a stile and continue parallel to the wall on the right. Go over the next stile and swing left to cross diagonally to a wall corner by a gate. Ignore the gate, instead following the outside of the wall to the right. You reach a stile and gate at a corner. Cross to enter a broad, walled way.

At the right bend ahead turn right. *A stile on the left here leads up to Alum Pot, a popular pothole, deep and dangerous. Even experienced potholers have lost their lives here in sudden floods, so don't go too close. This is on private land, so if you do visit, don't forget to call by Selside Farm and pay your small fee!*

Head down to join the road above Selside.

Turn left and walk up the road about 400 metres to a gate on the left signed **FP Sleights Rd**. Follow the broad green track as it rises diagonally right, up the field to a gate. *Looking down to your right, beyond the road, notice a number of small, rounded hills. These are* **drumlins** *– a glacial feature created when debris dropped by glaciers is subsequently scoured and smoothed.* Beyond, a faint track continues in the same line, through two more gates, to reach the edge of a rocky terrace by a wooded area. A path cuts up through the rocky outcrop to the left, towards a gate. Just before that gate, take another gate on the right, along a short enclosed track to a farm gate.

Through this, turn right to follow the wall on the left, heading north, all the way to **Colt Park**. *This was once a medieval lodge belonging to Furness Abbey, probably used, as the name suggests, to breed horses.*

If your destination is Ribblehead, then turn right beyond Colt Park farmhouse and follow the access lane down to the road. Turn left and continue to the T-junction. Here turn left to head up to the Station Inn at Ribblehead.

If your destination is Chapel-le-Dale, then go through the gate on the left, pass behind Colt Park farmhouse and along the wall on the left for 50 metres. A footpath cuts right, diagonally across the rough pasture. Take the faint track as it follows the contour around the foot of Park Fell, crossing another stile. *Down to the right, on the edge of the limestone plateau overlooking Ribblehead, the outline remains of a possible Viking or Anglo-Danish farmhouse can still be seen (SD765784).* Continue to cross two gates and a stile before swinging right to join Low Sleights Road. Turn left along the road (be very careful of fast moving traffic) and continue on to the Old Hill Inn.

(Above) Beside the river Ribble. (Below) Dropping into Crummack Dale.

© English Heritage Photographic Library

At the northern summit rim of Ingleborough, looking out over Whernside (top).

Reconstruction of Ingleborough hillfort as it may have been 2000 years ago. Celtic warriors approach via Swine Tail (right).

The final approach to the summit via Swine Tail (bottom).

Ingleborough Hillfort

On reaching the summit of Ingleborough you are met with a vast, flat, rock-strewn plateau. It is the size of eight football pitches and rises slightly to the north west. Amongst the jumble of rocks are modern structures - cairns and shelters built by walkers. Near the western end is a modern cruciform shelter and beyond that the derelict remnants of a Hospice tower, built and demolished in 1830.

But look carefully and you can still see the traces of much more ancient structures. Around the rim of the whole plateau are the remains of a wall or rampart. Across the mid-section, from north to south, is a series of faint circular features which are widely believed to be the remains of Iron Age huts. These are easiest to see at the southern end.

Ingleborough is traditionally thought to be the highest Iron Age hillfort in Britain, built by the Brigantes prior to the Roman invasion.

The hillfort was first recorded in 1855 by John Phillips in his book **The Rivers, Mountains and Seacoast of Yorkshire**. There was an accompanying detailed map drawn by the landowner James Farrer. Phillips concluded, **"Ingleborough was a great hill-fort of the Britons."** These structures have been described a number of times since, but never formally excavated.

In 1988 a survey of the site was conducted by the Royal Commission on the Historical Monuments of England (RCHME), following concerns about the erosion of the peak due to the huge number of walkers tackling the Three Peaks Challenge. They surveyed the entire site, recording the positions of 20 visible hut circles, varying in diameter from 5.5 m to 8.0 m. (see plan). They noted that

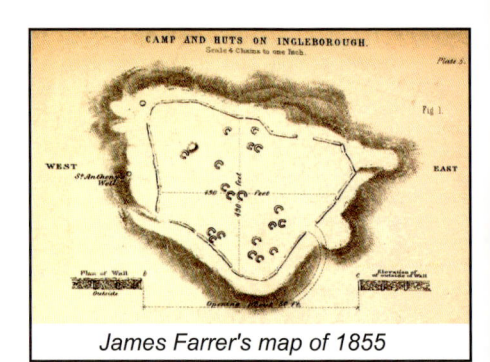

Circular feature, SE corner

James Farrer's map of 1855

most were at least partly turf covered and five appeared to have drainage gullies. Five appeared to have entrances and two showed evidence of previous excavation.

The rampart was recorded as being between 3.0 m to 5.0 m thick, the inside made of upstanding blocks and the outer face of drystone construction. It survives to a maximum height of 1.0 m internally and up to 3.0 m externally in the south east corner, but nowhere were the faces well preserved. Quarry scoops were noted on the inside. The rampart was missing entirely along much of the northern edge of the summit.

Part of the wall near the north east corner was subject to a more detailed survey, to investigate its unusual construction (Fig 2 on the plan). Upright through stones divide the rampart into boxes about 2 metres wide. Archaeologist Alan King, who has studied the site for a number of years, believes they may indicate a walkway on the rampart, or may be an attempt to copy techniques developed elsewhere with timber. He is in no doubt the site is that of an Iron Age hillfort.

The RCHME survey team concluded **" ... the site has been assumed to be a fort of the 1st millennium BC and in the absence of any evidence to the contrary this remains the most likely explanation. ... Given the relatively poor climate experienced during much of the Iron Age, especially in regard to the predominance of westerly winds, it is unlikely that the summit of Ingleborough was permanently occupied. Seasonal**

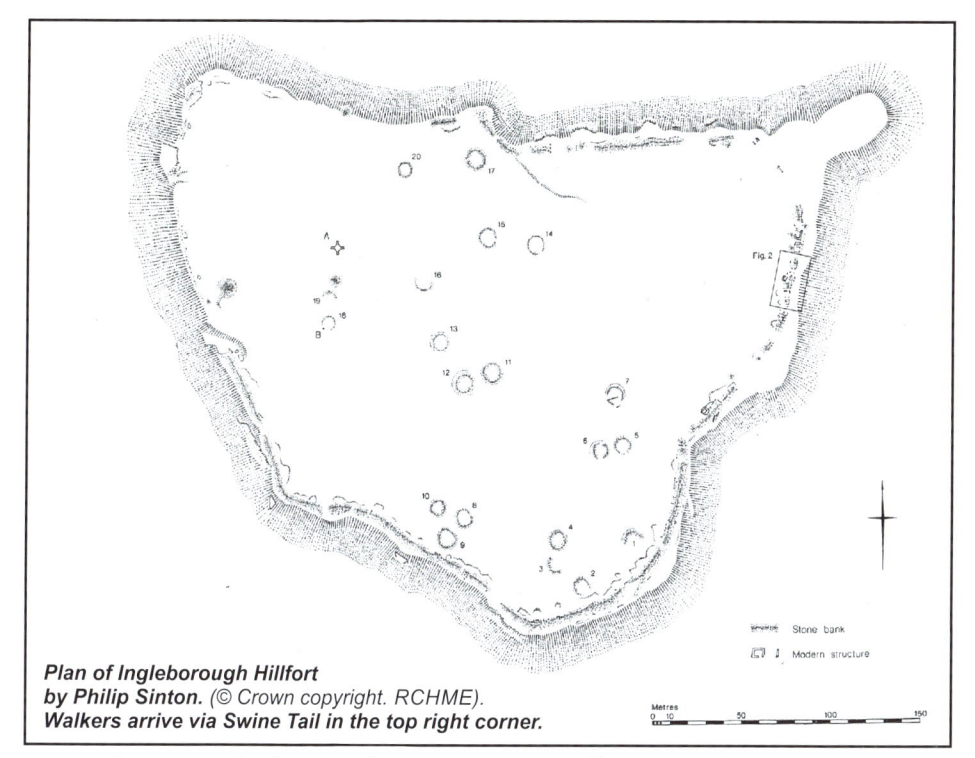

Plan of Ingleborough Hillfort by Philip Sinton. (© Crown copyright. RCHME). Walkers arrive via Swine Tail in the top right corner.

occupation as part of a transhumance cycle or a non-occupational role connected with the expression of prestige or social ritual seems to be indicated."

In recent years, however, this interpretation has been challenged by archaeologists like Yvonne Luke. She believes the structures are much older, dating back to the Bronze Age. She thinks the perimeter enclosure was never intended as a defensive structure and only really exists as a wall in the north-east corner. She argues that elsewhere it is an earth and stone embankment incorporating many gaps, with an unusual internal ditch not really adapted for defensive purposes. She thinks the circular features may not be huts at all, but ring cairns. These were the **chapels** of their day. She feels that the site is better described as a Bronze Age **hilltop sanctuary**.

Whatever the truth, there's no doubt that the construction would have required enormous resources and would indicate the site's huge cultural importance during prehistoric times.

Today Ingleborough peak is under pressure and the ancient remains with it. Between 1968 and 2000, the Pen-y-ghent café at Horton-in-Ribblesdale recorded over 200,000 people departing its doors to take on the Three Peaks Challenge.

Reconstruction of an Iron Age Roundhouse, National Museum of Wales

So, explore the mountain and its mysterious ancient structures, but tread lightly and leave this most beautiful and enigmatic mountain exactly as you find it.

WILDLIFE: This section of the walk includes riverbank, woodland and limestone pavement as well as the high ground of Ingleborough summit.

As you leave Settle the route follows the river Ribble where **Mallard** are common and **Goosander, Heron** and **Dipper** can be seen. In spring the aromatic displays of **Wild Garlic** are unmissable. In autumn attention should be on the water where you may be lucky enough to watch **Salmon** leaping at Langcliffe Weir and Stainforth Force as they make their way upstream to spawn - most common in late September and October.

The climb from Feizor passes Wharfe Wood, which is well worth a diversion for its spectacular spring flowers. **Bluebell, Wood Sorrel, Lady's Mantle, Meadowsweet** and **Betony** all grow in the rich verges of the lane out of Wharfe village.

Parts of Ingleborough have been designated as a National Nature Reserve because of the outstanding limestone pavement at Souther Scales and Sulber Nick, as well as both limestone and heather-rich acid grasslands. The limestone grassland supports **Early Purple Orchid, Wild Thyme** and **Bird's-foot-trefoil** making way for the mauve **Small Scabious** and **Harebell** later in the summer. **Common Rock-rose**, a delicate yellow flower, is the food plant of the caterpillar of the rare **Northern Brown Argus** butterfly.

The area is managed by grazing traditional breeds of cattle including **Blue Grey.** These native breeds are uniquely able to digest and live on a diet very low in nutrition and are better adapted to cope with the hostile upland climate. This regime has benefited wildflowers and in May delightful displays of **Bird's-eye Primrose** can be seen on the lower slopes.

Ribblehead quarry has been left to recolonise and in some areas water collects and has formed damp conditions where **Northern Spike-rush** grows, **Dragonfly** and **Damselfly** breed and **Oystercatcher, Lapwing, Redshank** and **Ringed Plover** visit.

Background photo: Deergrass (a sedge) grows in the acid grassland at the foot of Ingleborough.

(1) *Northern Brown Argus* (N.E.W.)   **(2)** *Meadowsweet* (JP)
(3) *Early Purple Orchid* (JP)   **(4)** *Bird's-eye Primrose* (JP)

(5) *Wild Thyme* (N.E.W.)   **(6)** *Harebell* (N.E.W.)
(7) *Common Rock-rose* (N.E.W.)   **(8)** *Bird's-foot-trefoil* (N.E.W.)

14. Simon Fell to Hill Inn (Chapel-le-Dale) *[4.0 miles]*

1.　The path is very easy to follow as it climbs steadily towards the summit. Across a stile the track becomes increasingly rocky underfoot as it rises across Simon Fell Breast with the summit of Ingleborough now tantalisingly close.

2.　At the foot of the final rocky peak the slope ahead is covered with boulders, but a well-laid stone stairway veers round to the right, climbing over a steep rocky edge. Care is needed here. Soon the path opens out onto the wide, flat top of Ingleborough.

Strewn with rocks, the plateau rises gently towards the west with views across the dale below, over Twistleton Scars to Morecambe Bay in the distance. The panoramic views are unsurpassed on a clear day. Turning northwards, the whale-back of Whernside dominates the view. In the distance, nestled between its peak and that of Great Coum behind it, sit the Howgills. Swinging north you see Wild Boar Fell, Mallerstang Edge and Great Shunner Fell. Continuing clockwise brings you to Cam Fell with the long body of Pen-y-ghent and Fountains Fell to its right.

In the centre of the plateau a cross-shaped windbreak makes a good place for a rest. On top of the pillar in the centre is a plate showing the surrounding peaks and sights. Be sure to take time and explore the ancient remains of Ingleborough hillfort.

3.　Retrace the way you came up to make the descent. As you climb down the stone pathway, a fork in the path leads left down a slabbed way to a gate.

4.　Through the gate the path drops to the left, along the route of a stream, to disappear over the edge. At first sight this is a hair-raising prospect, but with care the steep descent is made following a stone pathway that initially zig-zags down the steepest part, before dropping quickly to the foot by a wall corner. This is a tricky descent at any time, but extra care is needed with tired legs. It should be avoided in icy conditions.

If the destination is Ribblehead instead, then once through the gate a faint track continues ahead following the very edge of the ridge. This is a fine traverse, particularly in good weather, to cross the north western edge of Simon Fell and Park Fell. Follow the wall on your right to drop down, over a stile, to Colt Park and follow the access lane out onto the main road. Turn left and follow this down to the T-junction, where a left turn will bring you to the Station Inn at Ribblehead.

5.　Once down the steepest part, the path continues out from Humphrey Bottom and across Souther Scales Fell along a paved walkway, constructed to protect the path through the Ingleborough Nature Reserve from the boots of thousands of Three Peaks walkers. Wooden boardwalks cross boggy sections. Beyond a gate the path runs on better ground. *Soon you pass a large deep hole on the right of the path –* **Braithwaite Wife Hole** *– a natural shakehole or* **doline**, *formed by the dissolution of the limestone bedrock by a pool of weakly acidic water over a very long time*. You now drop between stunning limestone terraces. Swing right to follow an easy path along Souther Scales Scars.

6.　Eventually, just before you reach a gate signed **FP Sleights Rd**, a track cuts off to descend sharply to the left. This is a direct route to Chapel-le-Dale. The main path for the Hill Inn continues straight ahead through the gate. *Just before the next gate, another track leads up to the right alongside the wall to* **Great Douk Cave**, *which is worth a visit if time permits.*

The grassy path continues north to join Low Sleights Road at a gate. A left turn takes you down the road to the Old Hill Inn.

Angles and Vikings

The early medieval period following the departure of the Romans in 410 AD is traditionally called **The Dark Ages** because little is known of it. In the north, life probably continued pretty much as it had before, with small tribal chiefdoms developing.

By the late sixth century a new wave of settlers began to make their mark in the region. **Angles** came from Denmark and settled in the north, **Saxons** from Germany colonised the south. What began as a trickle soon became a flood and the Britons were forced to give way. Anglian place names in the district show the extent of their influence – Shipley, Ilkley, Addingham, Skipton, and Horton. Much of the north ended up as part of the Anglo-Saxon kingdom of Northumbria.

Around 800 AD new invaders arrived from Scandinavia – the **Vikings**. The **Danes** began raiding in the east, eventually bringing a huge army to take Northumbria as a Viking kingdom known as the Danelaw. The **Norsemen**, from Norway, made their way via Scotland and Ireland and came from the west. Gradually pushing inland they built their distinctive farmsteads in the upland landscape. Some 60% of placenames between Settle and Sedbergh are Scandinavian in origin. Many modern Dales words come straight from the Scandinavian – dale, gill, beck, crag, fell and scar.

A rare example of a Viking-age farmstead was discovered in 1964 on the limestone terrace at the foot of Park Fell, above Ribblehead (SD765784). Excavations revealed three buildings in an enclosure; the main dwelling was built in the style of a longhouse, with a workshop and kitchen. Amongst the finds were four Anglo-Saxon coins or stycas, one of which had been struck for Archbishop Wulfhere. They can be dated to around 850-875 AD and the position they were found means they date or pre-date the building. Whether this is an early Norse Viking farmstead, or more likely an Anglo-Danish settlement is unclear, but it seems to mark the area where the two influences from east and west met.

The southern doorway entrance to the main long building (above).

A computer model of what the farmstead might have looked like (below).

Aerial shot showing the location and layout of the farmstead.

(Above) Limestone pavement at Souther Scales (photo © Julia Pearson)
(Below) The Cumbrian Fellsman crosses Ribblehead Viaduct (photo © David Pratt).

Section 4
DENTDALE
Chapel-le-Dale to Sedbergh
15.7 miles

The entire route from Chapel-le-Dale into Dentdale follows an ancient packhorse trail called the Craven Way.

The path passes the tiny church of St Leonard's and along a lovely wooded track before turning to follow the eastern foot of Whernside.

There is the option to climb to the summit of Yorkshire's highest peak at Bruntscar, and in clear weather this might be hard to resist. Otherwise the way continues under the stunning Ribblehead Viaduct, past the lonely signal box at Blea Moor, before climbing to cross the northern flank of Whernside. At Wold End, Dentdale opens out ahead, perhaps the most beautiful of all the Yorkshire Dales.

Deepdale Beck and the river Dee lead gently into the charming village of Dent, once the major town in the region and a place to linger. Finally another ancient packhorse trail climbs over to Longstone Fell and Frostrow and on to Sedbergh – England's official Book Town.

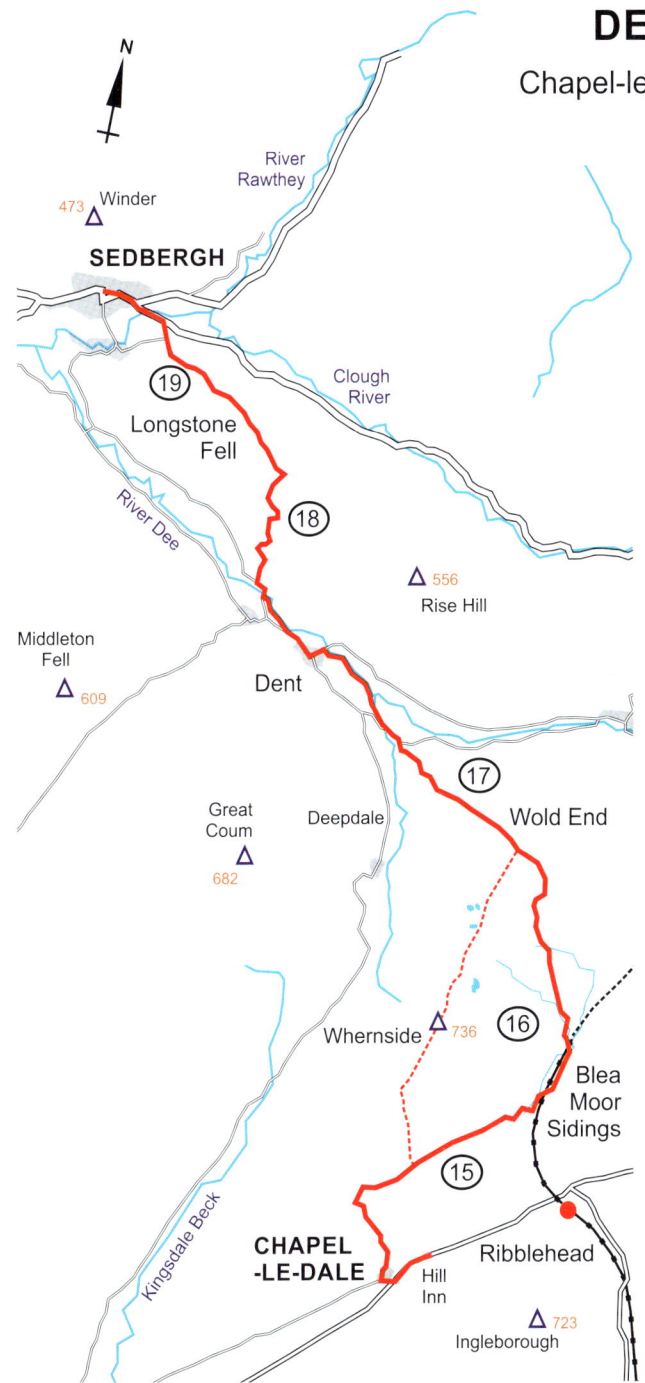

65

15. Hill Inn (Chapel-le-Dale) to Blea Moor Sidings *[3.7 miles]*

1. From the Hill Inn set off down the road in a southerly direction.

*Almost immediately Philpin Lane cuts back on the right. This is the **Three Peaks** route from Bruntscar and can be taken as a short cut if time is pressing. Though much less interesting than the main route, it cuts a mile off the distance.*

Continue down the road, passing the old schoolhouse – now bunkhouse accommodation for larger parties. The road drops to the turn-off for the tiny hamlet of **Chapel-le-Dale** on the right. Follow the road to St Leonard's Church.

Here are buried the remains of over 200 men, women and children – the navvies and their families who helped build the Settle-Carlisle railway between 1870 and 1877 and perished through accident or disease. There are memorials both inside and outside the church.

2. Turn right past the church to climb a narrow lane. Just beyond the church on the right is Hurtle Pot, a deep hole that can be reached through a gate round to the right above it. *The pothole itself can only be explored underwater, but it was here that a sculpture by modernist Charles L'Anson, seen a little way further on, was unceremoniously dumped in 1983!*

3. Ahead the path forks. Follow the right hand track for Eller Beck. This rises along a very pleasant wooded lane, passing the rescued L'Anson sculpture. Just beyond Gill Head farm the lane opens out and heads towards the southern rim of Whernside. Where the waters of Ellerbeck Gill cross the path as it swings right, follow the track, signed **Deepdale**, up to Ellerbeck farm.

4. Pass through a gate into the farm yard, swinging right through two more gates to follow the track as it drops towards wooded crags and on to Bruntscar. *This is a quiet, beautiful place between the twin mountain ranges of Whernside and Ingleborough with fine views up the dale to Ribblehead viaduct.*

5. After passing some farm buildings at Bruntscar Hall (built in 1689), the main track splits by a lime kiln. The right track heads down to the Old Hill Inn and is the Three Peaks route. The other swings sharp left to head straight up the mountainside.

*Here there is an option to take the route over the top of Whernside. The ascent is steep and hard work, but in clear weather it is hard to resist. This route cuts a mile from the overall distance, but is paid for in the burning of extra energy and tired legs **(see box for details)**.*

The main route onwards, however, has its own charms and rewards and if it's misty atop the mountain then don't hesitate and continue straight ahead through the gate for **Winterscales**. A faint track now crosses more open fields but the route is easy to follow, passing through a number of gates to reach Ivescar. Here several farm gates have to be negotiated before continuing along the same line to Winterscales Farm. Ignore the track dropping right and continue across a cattle grid to pass the farm.

6. At Winterscales the path drops right to cross a humped footbridge signposted **Whernside**. Pass through a gate beyond a barn to bear left and follow the stream up towards the signal box.

7. The track now swings right, away from the stream to pass under the railway line. Turn left to follow the path along the rail track for **Dent**. *Those who took the optional route to Ribblehead rejoin the main route here.* Pass the lonely outpost of Blea Moor signalbox and the accompanying house and continue north between beck and rail.

16. Blea Moor Sidings to Wold End
[3.4 miles]

1.　The track north from Blea Moor signal box crosses the beck at a couple of spots, finally making use of a wooden footbridge to cross a tributary before swinging in to cross the railway line by an aqueduct that carries the waters of Force Gill Beck across the line. *Shortly after passing under the aqueduct, the railway line disappears into Blea Moor tunnel for a long stretch under the moor before reappearing at the head of Dentdale. Its route can be followed over the fell top, marked by a series of spoil heaps and ventilation shafts.*

2.　Once across the aqueduct the main path rises steeply, heading for **Dentdale**. The rocky path continues up by the wall on the left, passing through a gate and continuing upwards. *Here there are fine views of the final waterfall in a series that cascades down from above Greensett Crags on the eastern flank of Whernside.* Halfway up the track, beyond the waterfalls, a stile on the left leads onto the long Three Peaks route up to the top of **Whernside**. Ignore this and continue to climb straight up for **Deepdale**, through a gate where the ground begins to level out. *The views back across Greensett Crags below Whernside to Ingleborough and Pen-y-ghent in the distance give a panorama of all three Dales peaks.*

3.　The path now heads north along a lovely broad green track. This is easy, pleasant walking. Excellent distant views over Dentdale open up ahead and to the right. As the path swings right to meet a ruined barn, the land ahead drops away into upper Dentdale.

The railway viaduct above Arten Gill can be seen in the distance as the railway curves around on the slopes of Wold Fell and Knoutberry Hill. Further round to the left the western flank of Rise Hill climbs up and beyond lies the lofty heights of Baugh Fell.

4.　This ancient packhorse track – known as the **Craven Way** – continues in its splendid isolation to curve left around Great Wold to finally meet the walls of a series of sheep folds, where the optional route from Whernside drops down past the tarns to rejoin the main path as a walled lane.

5.　The path becomes rockier as the walled lane descends past Rigg End and Dentdale reveals itself in all its beauty as it opens up ahead.

Optional route over Whernside

The track climbs steeply, passing through two gates before reaching the wall along the ridge. Turn right and follow the path as it climbs gently, following the wall, to the summit. The trig point is on the other side, beside a shelter. As the highest of the Three Peaks, the panoramic views are magnificent, on those occasions when the mountain top is not shrouded in mist.

The route continues along the ridge, now beginning to drop. As you pass Greensett Tarn below on the right, just before the path begins to drop more steeply, watch out for a wall corner on the left, which gives way to a fence. A makeshift stile allows you to cross the fence and follow a faint track as it leads north, pulling gently away from the fence. The track is indistinct in places, and wet underfoot, but continues in a straight line to drop past Whernside Tarns, a place of great solitude and calm. The track, now much clearer, turns slightly north east, passing well to the right of the two prominent cairns ahead, to meet the corner wall of a sheep fold. Continue, with the wall on the left, to descend and join the main path at **Boot of the Wold** (*Part 16, para 5*).

Force Gill in winter

Dropping into Dentdale

Fell Running: This tradition was born from the competitive banter of local sheep fairs in the early nineteenth century. With the increasing demands for wool from the mill towns of Yorkshire and Lancashire, these fairs became bigger, more important social occasions involving the whole community. A tradition of short fast races from the show ground grew, with local guides and shepherds showing their speed, fitness and knowledge of the fells.

A different amateur tradition of mountain running emerged after the second world war. Much longer, stamina based events developed, like the **Lake District Mountain Marathon Trial** in 1952 and the famous **Yorkshire Three Peaks Fell Race** in 1954. From small beginnings these events grew and became more popular so that by the mid 1970s thousands would apply to enter **The Peaks,** as it is affectionately known. Whilst walkers are thought to have done well if they complete the gruelling 24 mile circuit in less than 12 hours, the top runners finish in under three.

The sport continues to thrive with the Fell Runners Association enjoying a membership of over 6000. There are now around 600 races a year, from three-mile hill sprints to epics over 24 lung-bursting miles.

Fell runners tackle Whernside from Dent

Looking back to the summit from Whernside Tarns on the optional route

17. Wold End to Dent *[3.2 miles]*

1. The walled track continues down and west. It's hard to take your eyes from the magnificent view of the green pastures of Dentdale ahead, but the going underfoot is increasingly rocky. *Beyond the western brow of Rise Hill the green and brown layered folds of the Howgills beckon.*

2. Finally, beyond a stile and gate, the walled lane opens up and the track continues between a fence and a wall on the right. *To the left Deepdale closes in to join up with Dentdale coming from the right ahead. The magnificent peak of Great Coum towers on the left, which at 687 metres almost matches Pen-y-ghent. Beyond that the land dips into Barbondale, before climbing again to Middleton Fell.* The track here has been improved and it's an easy walk down towards Whernside Manor. The track now drops between walls to turn left through a gate and out onto a road.

3. The road drops steeply to the right through woods. The bubbling Deepdale Beck can be heard but not seen as the road descends to join the main road leading to Dent, by a converted chapel on the left. Turn left along the main road to cross the beck at Bridge End.

4. Immediately across the road bridge, a footpath marked **FP to Church Bridge** turns off to the right. This is the Dales Way route into Dent and you follow it along Deepdale Beck all the way.

5. The path is narrow but easy to follow, passing through numerous gates along the way. The beck eventually joins the river Dee by a footbridge and ford and the path continues as a raised track above the riverside. As you approach Dent itself, the path veers away from the river to cross another tributary stream at a footbridge, before swinging sharp right by the sports field to rejoin the river at Church Bridge.

6. Stop by the bridge. This is a nice spot for a break. The route continues into Dent village, or optionally you can continue to follow the Dales Way along the riverside by crossing the road through 2 tiny stiles.

7. The main route follows the road up into Dent village, passing the blacksmith's to swing right around the huge 12th century church of St. Andrew and into the narrow cobbled streets that make Dent so special.

18. Dent to Longstone Fell *[3.0 miles]*

1.   Follow the main road through Dent, passing the two pubs, the school, car park and Heritage Centre to leave the village. Eventually the river closes in on the right. Pass through a gate signed for **Barth Bridge** to rejoin the riverside and the **Dales Way** route for a little while.

2.   The riverside walk is easy and pleasant here. Eventually climb some stone steps up to Barth Bridge and turn right, following the road across the bridge. The road swings left, but ignore the two lanes immediately on the right and continue along the road for a short way, about 100 metres.

3.   Turn up the next lane rising on the right, crossing Blea Beck Gill. The narrow lane rises steeply, before swinging left at a junction to pass Hole House Cottage. Continue along the lane as it swings right and rises again. Ignore the next left but take the one after to climb up to Lunds Farm.

4.   At Lunds Farm go through the gate into the farmyard. Turn sharp left, through another gate before a barn, then right through a series of gates into a walled lane. *This is a working farm and this gated area is used for penning sheep, so be prepared to be diverted through an adjoining field if required.* The lane rises, here stony, narrow and sometimes wet, before opening out into a wider walled way. If possible, follow this as it swings right and left, rising to a double gate before continuing as a muddy path alongside the wall on your right.

5.   However, if the way ahead has become impassable, particularly after heavy rain, a ladder stile over the wall on the left leads to an open, rough field. Here head straight up the hill, north. There is no visible track, but the going underfoot is much better. Keep the wall to the right in sight as it swings first away then back to rejoin you. Negotiate a way between a few large shake holes and head up to the right field corner where a gate on the right leads back onto the original track.

6.   The way now continues to rise, with the wall on your left, as a fine open green track. *The view back across Dentdale is lovely and the Howgills slip into view ahead.* Eventually cross a stile ahead and turn left to follow the wall as it rises to the hill brow. *Here the view of the Howgills is magnificent.*

7.   As the wall turns left, the track continues straight on, dropping gently to join Holebeck Gill below on the right. *You are about to cross the line of the Dent Fault, but alas there are no clear signs on the ground.*

DENT is dominated by St. Andrew's Church which dates from the 12th century. The village has plenty of B&Bs, two pubs and several campsites. There's an annual music festival, a local arts and craft scene and a visit to the Heritage Centre is a must.

Mist descends on the fells above Dent

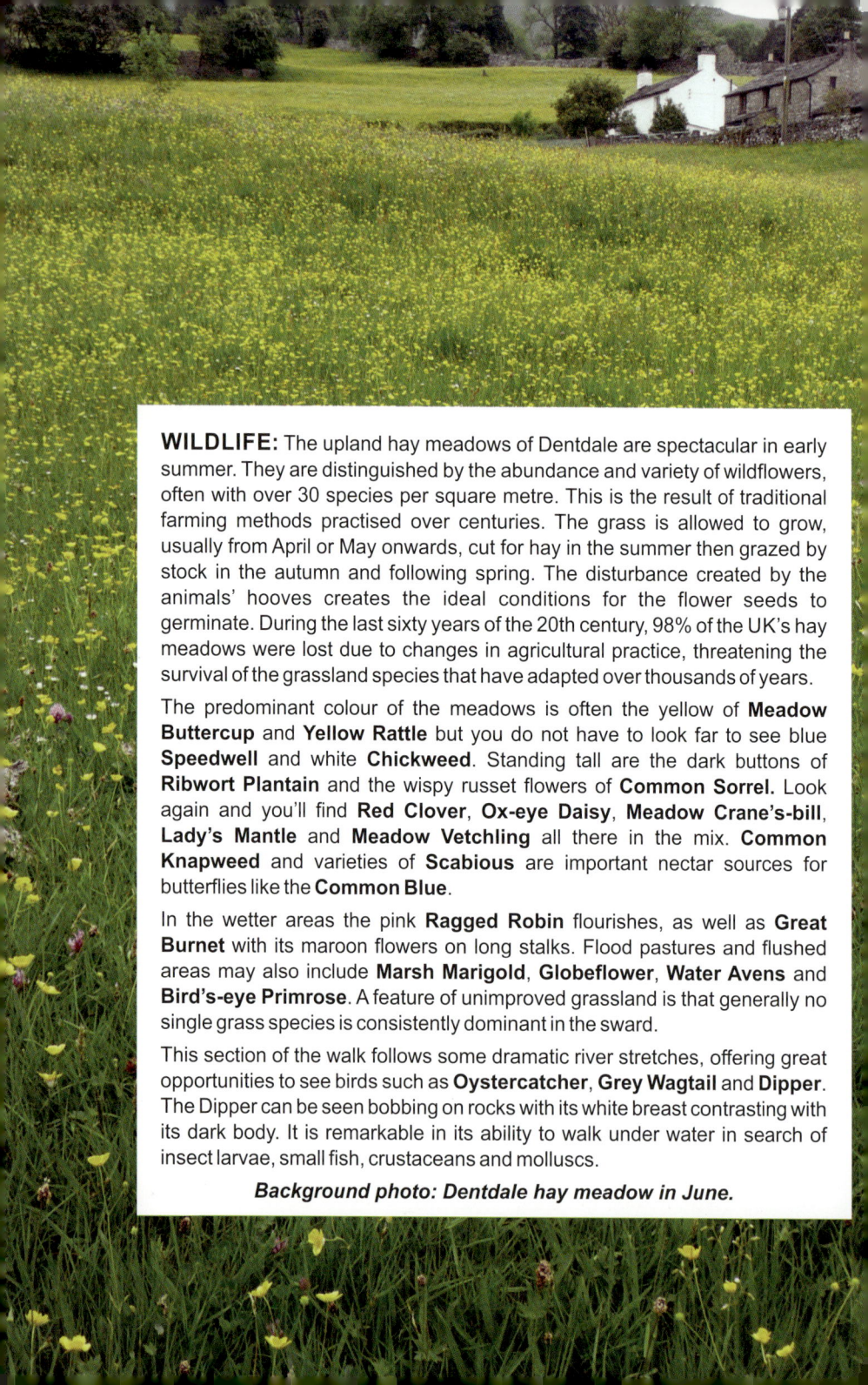

WILDLIFE: The upland hay meadows of Dentdale are spectacular in early summer. They are distinguished by the abundance and variety of wildflowers, often with over 30 species per square metre. This is the result of traditional farming methods practised over centuries. The grass is allowed to grow, usually from April or May onwards, cut for hay in the summer then grazed by stock in the autumn and following spring. The disturbance created by the animals' hooves creates the ideal conditions for the flower seeds to germinate. During the last sixty years of the 20th century, 98% of the UK's hay meadows were lost due to changes in agricultural practice, threatening the survival of the grassland species that have adapted over thousands of years.

The predominant colour of the meadows is often the yellow of **Meadow Buttercup** and **Yellow Rattle** but you do not have to look far to see blue **Speedwell** and white **Chickweed**. Standing tall are the dark buttons of **Ribwort Plantain** and the wispy russet flowers of **Common Sorrel**. Look again and you'll find **Red Clover**, **Ox-eye Daisy**, **Meadow Crane's-bill**, **Lady's Mantle** and **Meadow Vetchling** all there in the mix. **Common Knapweed** and varieties of **Scabious** are important nectar sources for butterflies like the **Common Blue**.

In the wetter areas the pink **Ragged Robin** flourishes, as well as **Great Burnet** with its maroon flowers on long stalks. Flood pastures and flushed areas may also include **Marsh Marigold**, **Globeflower**, **Water Avens** and **Bird's-eye Primrose**. A feature of unimproved grassland is that generally no single grass species is consistently dominant in the sward.

This section of the walk follows some dramatic river stretches, offering great opportunities to see birds such as **Oystercatcher**, **Grey Wagtail** and **Dipper**. The Dipper can be seen bobbing on rocks with its white breast contrasting with its dark body. It is remarkable in its ability to walk under water in search of insect larvae, small fish, crustaceans and molluscs.

Background photo: Dentdale hay meadow in June.

(1) Meadow Crane's-bill (N.E.W.)   *(2) Speedwell & Daisy (JP)*
(3) Common Sorrel (JP)   *(4) Yellow Rattle (N.E.W.)*

(5) Common Blue butterfly on Scabious (JP.)   *(6) Oystercatcher (N.E.W.)*
(7) Dipper (N.E.W.)   *(8) Grey Wagtail (N.E.W.)*

19. Longstone Fell to Sedbergh [2.4 miles]

1. The track continues with Holebeck Gill deepening on the right. Eventually the gill swings away to the right, continuing north, while your track heads north west.

2. The track here can be faint in places and wet underfoot as it continues over the northern flank of Frostrow Fells, heading straight towards the peak of Winder at the south western end of the Howgill range.

3. The track continues to drop towards a wall on the right, before leading down to join a walled farm lane via a ladder stile by a gate.

4. The route now is easy; simply follow the lane all the way to the main road.

5. Eventually the lane leads to the A684, which can be busy at times. Turn left and follow the main road, but take great care as there is no footpath. The road rises and swings right at a dangerous sharp corner to cross New Bridge. Just beyond, an optional footpath on the left, *Sedbergh avoiding road* offers a safer route parallel to the road.

6. This road then joins the A683 at a T-junction. Straight ahead, above the houses and between two hills, the remains of the Norman castle mound at Castlehaw can be seen in the trees. The roadside path can be followed left, all the way into Sedbergh.

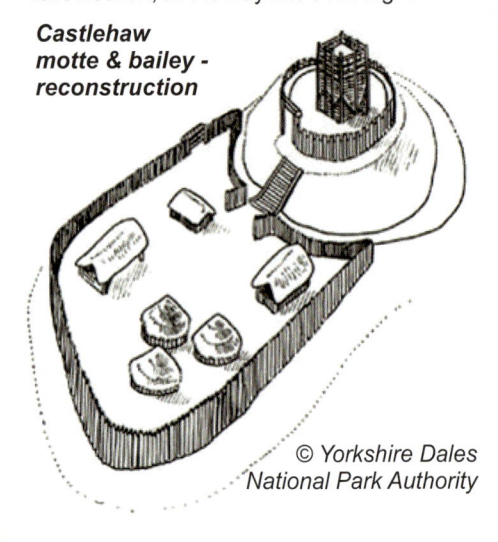

Castlehaw motte & bailey - reconstruction

© Yorkshire Dales National Park Authority

Dropping from Frostrow, Sedbergh awaits ahead at the foot of Winder

74

The Harrying of the North

The Anglo-Saxon reign came to an end with the Norman invasion and the victory of William the Conqueror at the Battle of Hastings in 1066.

After consolidating his position in the south, William turned his attention to the rebellious north. With a cruelty that shocked even his staunchest supporters, William unleashed what can best be described as a genocide. Many thousands were put to death: men, women, children, guilty or innocent, it mattered not. For those that escaped the slaughter, their homes and crops were burnt, leaving only famine in a ravaged landscape. One estimate of the time put the final death toll at 100,000. This was the Harrying of the North.

By 1089, when William had the country's assets listed in the Domesday Book, much of the north was recorded as *"waste"*.

Extract from the Domesday book

"In Swinden, Hellifield, Malham and Coniston [Cold] there are 13 and a half caracutes taxable.
Bjornulfr had the manors. Now William de Percy has [them] and they are waste".
(1 caracute is approximately 50 hectares)

William then carved the whole country up between himself and just 190 barons: names like Ilbert de Lacey, William de Percy, Robert de Mowbray, Robert de Romille, creating a legacy that survives in part to this day. For these barons the north was fit for hunting and little else.

The Norman barons stamped their authority on the region by building castles. The one at **Castlehaw**, Sedbergh, may well have been the northernmost such castle when it was built, the Scottish border lying just north of the Howgills at that time. Like the others it was constructed of wood, on a **motte and bailey** design.

The castles further north were built later by the Conqueror's son, William II (also known as Rufus). He pushed the Scottish border beyond Carlisle in 1092. Many of the castles were later rebuilt in stone, but not Castlehaw. All that remains now is the castle mound, but it is well worth the short diversion to explore.

The Norman barons in turn gave land generously to the French monastic orders, in return for the promise of a quick entrance to paradise in the hereafter.

The monks sought the wild, isolated landscape to build their abbeys – Rievaulx, Kirkstall, Jervaux, Furness and Fountains. The Cistercians brought their skills in handling sheep from their home at Clairvaulx in France and were soon rearing sheep across the Yorkshire Dales on a massive scale. Fountains had over a million acres in the Craven area, with estates as far as the Lake District. They shared the moors of Malhamdale with the Augustinian monks of Bolton Priory.

As well as extensive estates in Cumbria and Lancashire, Furness Abbey held land around Ribblehead, including Bruntscar, Ivescar, Winterscales and Colt Park. It also held land in Craven, including Flasby, Hetton and Gargrave, managed from a Grange at Winterburn. These holdings led inevitably to disputes with the monks at Fountains. By the time of their suppression, Fountains and Furness were the richest Cistercian monasteries in England.

The monks retained their powerful and ruthless grip on the land for 400 years, until the Dissolution of the Monasteries in 1539 by Henry VIII.

Adam Sedgwick

Walk along the cobbled main street of Dent and you can't miss the huge granite fountain, built by the local residents to commemorate their most famous son – the geologist Adam Sedgwick.

He was born in 1785, son of the Dent vicar. He went on to study mathematics, classics and theology at Trinity College, Cambridge. Winning a fellowship in 1810 gave him a degree of independence and he was ordained a deacon in 1817. The following year he was elected Woodwardian Professor of Geology, even though as he said himself, *"I knew absolutely nothing of geology"*.

He quickly became an active researcher, however, carrying out important field research all over Britain, in what was known as the **Heroic Age of Geology**.

In 1650 the former Archbishop of Armagh, James Ussher, taking the biblical record as literal truth, had pronounced that the earth was created on 22 October 4004 BC. Even in Sedgwick's time, most geologists were obsessed by reconciling the geological record with the biblical version of Noah's flood.

But Sedgwick's scientific approach proved the great antiquity of the earth's rocks. He decoded the complex geology of Lakeland, where he became friends with Wordsworth. In Wales he studied the oldest rocks known, belonging to an age he called the **Cambrian Period** (over 488 million years ago). They contained the earliest fossils so far discovered – recording the early stages of life on the planet.

He was accompanied on his Welsh field research for a time by one of his students, **Charles Darwin**. Learning of the vast periods of time it took for geological change helped Darwin formulate his own ideas.

The granite fountain memorial to Adam Sedgwick in Dent Main St.

When Darwin published his theory, ***On The Origin of the Species***, however, Sedgwick was appalled. He wrote to Darwin; *"I have read your book with more pain than pleasure. Parts of it I admired greatly; parts I laughed at till my sides were almost sore; other parts I read with absolute sorrow; because I think them utterly false & grievously mischievous..."*

Sedgwick's most loved work is ***A Memorial by the Trustees of Cowgill Chapel*** published in 1868. It was intended to correct an error by the church authorities in registering the name of the new chapel and to this end was ultimately successful, though it required the intervention of Queen Victoria and an act of Parliament. The bulk of the pamphlet, however, is taken up by a series of appendices *"on the climate, history and dialects of Dent"* and here we find Sedgwick's unique nineteenth century record of his beloved Dentdale. Sedgwick died just five years later, aged 88.

The Dent Fault: The western edge of the Carboniferous limestone landscape of the Dales is marked by the Dent Fault. Beyond lie the older Silurian bedrocks of Lakeland. Towards the end of the Carboniferous Period, around 290 million years ago, the rocks of the Lake District were uplifted, possibly by as much as 2.5 km above those of the Pennines, bringing the ancient basement rocks to the surface.

The Dent Fault runs from a point east of Kirkby Lonsdale in the south, along the valley of Barbondale and cuts across Dentdale just west of Barth Bridge. It goes on over Longstone Fell where the route of ***A Dales High Way*** crosses it, unseen, at a spot by Holebeck Gill marked as **Springs** on the OS map (SD 689 905). The first sign of a change appears where the Silurian sandstone is exposed in the streambed at the foot of Frostrow, just before entering the lane at Side farm.

The fault line continues north to cross the river Clough in Garsdale. Here a 1.5 km walk called **The Sedgwick Geological Trail** has been created (guide leaflets available from Sedbergh Information & Book Centre). The fault goes on to cross the western flank of Baugh Fell to Rawthey Bridge, then follows the line of the A683 to Kirkby Stephen.

The Dent Fault was discovered in the early 1820s by Adam Sedgwick as he studied the Cumbrian mountains and neighbouring areas. He believed it to be a continuation of the Craven Faults and called it **the Great Dislocations** when he published his paper in 1836.

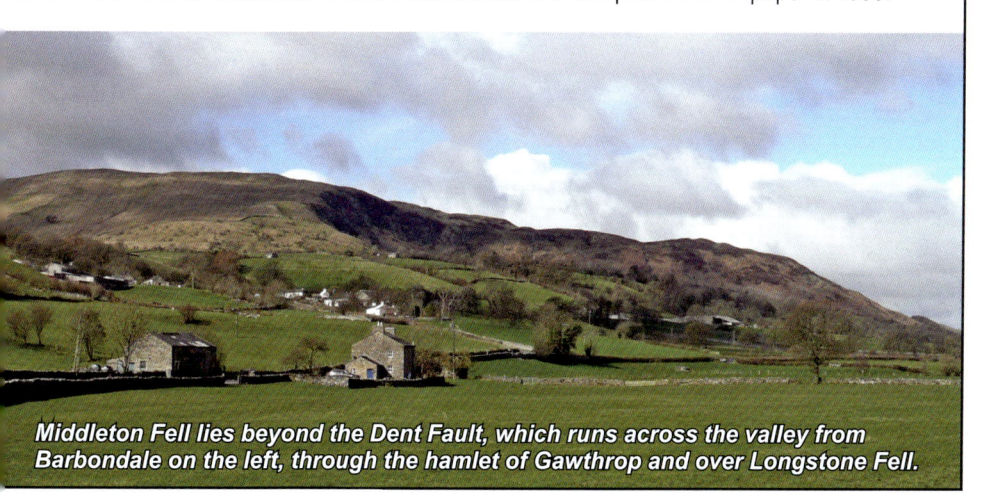

Middleton Fell lies beyond the Dent Fault, which runs across the valley from Barbondale on the left, through the hamlet of Gawthrop and over Longstone Fell.

The Changing Dales

Chris grew up on a small hill farm in upper Dentdale, with her brother Ian and parents John and Nancy Murdoch. The farm had 60 acres around the house, known as *inbye* land. The rest was fell, including a 250 acre *allotment* and the right to graze 100 sheep on Whernside.

Chris at home on the farm

"May 1965. The rent went up from £290 to £315 a year. Twenty five pounds a year may seem very little today but to a tenant farmer in Dentdale in the 1960s it took some finding. My family had lived at Stonehouse for nearly five years. My mum's meticulous records show that we had 325 breeding ewes, eight milk cows, four goats and 90 hens. Although Stonehouse was a sheep farm, the cows and hens were essential. The income from milk and eggs was regular with cheques arriving every month, unlike the sale of lambs and wool which happened once a year, in September."

1965 was a fairly typical year, with sheep sales bringing in £1,017, cattle £336, milk £726, wool £183 and the sale of a dog £30. Lambs fetched an average £4-4s-5d a head (about £78.50 at today's value). Around a quarter of the total farm income came in subsidies of one sort or another. Expenses included £378 on new stock and haulage, £172 on machinery and repairs, £112 on vets bills and a whopping £1,041 on animal feed. That is why hay making was so crucial.

"It was a wonderful childhood. My brother and I were farm children, born and brought up in the countryside and always outdoors. Not playing out exactly, more helping out – like all the other kids in the dale we had jobs to do on the farm. I fed hens, collected eggs, brought cows in for milking. I loved lambing time and clipping and sheep sales but wasn't too keen on hay time. For weeks before the first grass was cut our hands were rubbed with methylated spirits to "harden them up". Not that it worked - after a day in the hayfield turning grass with a rake, its wooden shaft sliding between fingers and thumbs, small hands were blistered and sore. The work was a relentless race against the weather to store feed for the following winter and everyone had to muck in. In the days before balers were seen in the Dales, hay was brought to the barns loose on a trailer or sledge and forked in through a forking hole. As the smallest in the family my job was inside the barn on the "hay mew", receiving the fork loads and spreading them out."

After deductions for essential household expenses such as groceries and fuel, the farm made a profit of just £260-18s-6d - a little less than £4,860 at today's (2017) value.

Today haymaking is done by machine and farmers cross the fells on quad bikes rather than by foot, but hill farming remains a precarious way to make a living. Net business income for hill farmers fell from £17,459 in 2004 to £10,786 in 2008, a figure that remained unchanged in 2014. The average age of a hill farmer is now 59. With these pressures many choose to sell up. Since 1954 the number of farms in the Dales National Park has fallen by a third and the number of small farms under 50 hectares (124 acres) has halved.

"When I wasn't helping on the farm, my school holidays were spent packing orders in Batty's shop in Dent. The dales women would write down their weekly grocery orders and these were packed in the shop and delivered to the farms by

van. Batty's was one of two grocers in the village. The other was Dinsdale's, which still exists as Dent Stores. There was also a post office, draper, butcher, cobbler, blacksmith, provender merchant, two pubs and two banks."

The post office closed in 2008 leaving just one shop remaining. The delivery vans to be seen trundling down the narrow roads to the village today are from supermarkets in Kendal and Lancaster. The two pubs are still open though, with a third at Cow Dub further up the dale. Dent also has its own brewery now. There are several campsites which are very busy in summer. The leisure industry is now vital to Dentdale's economy.

Dentdale's first census in 1801 revealed a population of 1,773, but the industrial revolution led to a rapid decline. However, there has been a steady growth since the sixties. A recent survey for the Dentdale Parish Plan in 2008 showed a population of 700 occupying 397 properties. One in five households, however, were second homes or holiday lets. Half the residents had lived there less than 10 years. Over 40% were retired. One of the major problems facing Dentdale is affordable housing.

"My parents farmed at Stonehouse for nearly 25 years. The years immediately prior to dad's retirement were an anxious time. Retiring from farming meant losing the house and the growth of second home ownership had pushed up the price of cottages in the dale. In the early 80s however, the National Park allowed a housing association to build five houses for rental purchase for first time home owners who lived or worked in Dentdale. In February 1985 my mum and dad moved the five miles into the village and happily lived out the rest of their lives in the dale that they both loved so much."

The Yorkshire Dales continue to evolve. Today tourism and leisure are key to its sustainability. Walkers who spend a night at a local B&B or campsite, buy a meal in the pub or cafe and stock up at the local store become part of the life of the modern Dales and help ensure its future.

John Murdoch feeds his sheep *(photo © Eliza & John Forder)*

The Howgill Fells from Frostrow

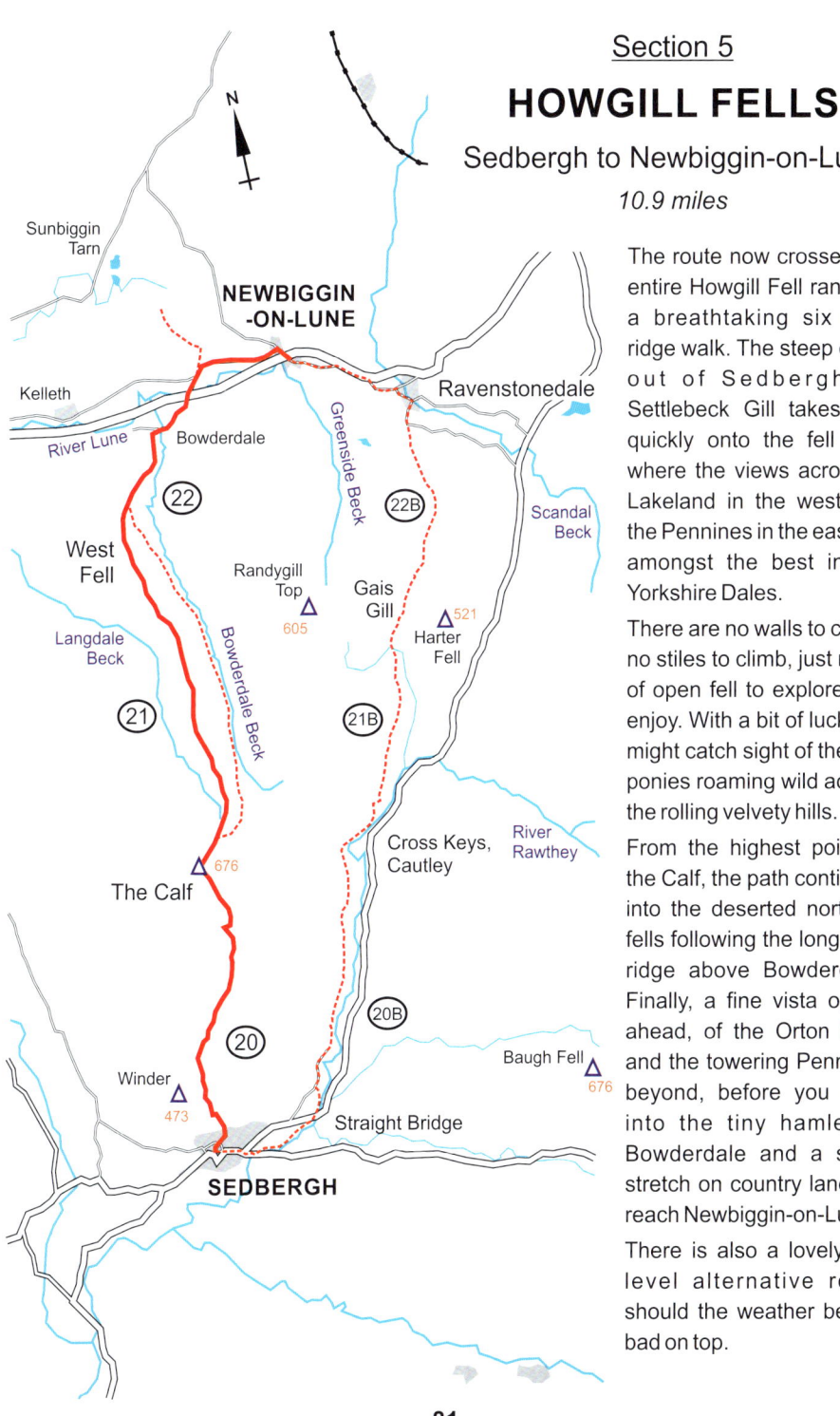

Section 5
HOWGILL FELLS
Sedbergh to Newbiggin-on-Lune
10.9 miles

The route now crosses the entire Howgill Fell range in a breathtaking six mile ridge walk. The steep climb out of Sedbergh up Settlebeck Gill takes you quickly onto the fell tops where the views across to Lakeland in the west and the Pennines in the east are amongst the best in the Yorkshire Dales.

There are no walls to cross, no stiles to climb, just miles of open fell to explore and enjoy. With a bit of luck you might catch sight of the Fell ponies roaming wild across the rolling velvety hills.

From the highest point at the Calf, the path continues into the deserted northern fells following the long high ridge above Bowderdale. Finally, a fine vista opens ahead, of the Orton Fells and the towering Pennines beyond, before you drop into the tiny hamlet of Bowderdale and a short stretch on country lanes to reach Newbiggin-on-Lune.

There is also a lovely low level alternative route should the weather be too bad on top.

Sedbergh Main Street

20. Sedbergh to the Calf *[3.6 miles]*

1. From the Main Street head uphill along Joss Lane, passing the main car park on the right. Towards the top of the hill the road swings right and is marked **To the Fells**. As it climbs north east, the lane narrows and finally reaches a gate into a farmyard. Pass through the gate and follow the track signed **FP to Fell** as it crosses the yard and swings left to pass through a gate into a narrow walled way. *Down to the right, just across a field, the mound of Castlehaw is prominent and can be reached by a short diversion through a gate on the right.*

2. Finally the way opens out to pass through a gate onto the open fell. The foot of Winder rises sharply ahead to the left and the deep ravine of Settlebeck Gill cuts to the right. This is a beautiful sight. There are several tracks heading off, including a clear green track rising diagonally left up Winder. But follow instead a rougher track that sticks close to the edge of the beck ravine as it climbs steeply ahead. The track follows the route of a tributary stream before eventually crossing it. A well walked track swings left to follow the left foot of the dale, but keep to a fainter track following close to the ravine edge, now high above the beck.

3. Follow the track as it heads up to the ridge ahead and swings right to join the main path from Winder heading towards Calders. *The views across to the east, of Baugh Fell and back to Frostrow, Middleton Fell and Whernside are excellent.* The main path gently rises to the right of the peak of Arant Haw.

4. Now the view to the west opens out. *Beyond the lovely folds of the Howgill ridges, the eastern Lakeland Fells rise.*

5. The path is now easy to follow. A fence to the right marks the very steep drop over Hobdale Gill and guides the path to the final major climb to the peak of Calders, which is only slightly lower than the Calf.

6. There is now a fine ridge walk, punctuated only by a short drop before the final push up to the trig point that marks the summit of the Calf. This is a busy spot in fine weather, but also an excellent place for a break beside the tarn. *The panoramic views here are amongst the finest in the country!*

Civil War and the Quakers

By the 17th century religion was playing an increasingly significant role in political and social development. Henry VIII's reformation had led to the break with Rome and the foundation of the Church of England, but these changes didn't go nearly as far as the growing Protestant movement demanded. They were fundamentalists – **Puritans** - opposed to the trappings of the High Church.

Following the Dissolution of the Monasteries, Dales people had generally prospered. Many of the wooden houses began to be rebuilt in stone. The old Norman barons had given way to the new landed gentry. The Cliffords of Skipton were now joined by the Bellasis, Wentworths, Cholmleys and Fairfaxes. Many had bought into the nobility and now held seats in parliament.

Charles 1, however, believed in the divine right of kings to rule. He was on a collision course with Parliament. In 1642, he withdrew to York and civil war loomed.

People's loyalties were split in complex ways, but in the end divisions were mostly resolved on religious lines: Catholics and Anglicans for Royalty, Puritans for Parliament. Most of the leading gentry, including the Cliffords, went with the King. The yeomen and artisans of the day were increasingly politicised and supported Parliament. The labourers and peasants were pressed into the service of whoever their landlord supported.

At first things went the way of the Royalists in the north, with most major towns being taken. When Bradford fell in July 1643, only Hull remained in Parliamentary hands. Fortunes changed in 1644 when Oliver Cromwell and his Roundheads came to relieve Hull. The Royalists were defeated at Marston Moor and York surrendered. When Skipton Castle fell to Parliament in 1645 the north was lost.

Throughout this period a young Puritan called **George Fox** wandered across the war-torn landscape in a state of mental torment and confusion, seeking spiritual understanding.

It was a time of intense political and social turmoil, with movements such as the **Levellers** and the **Diggers** struggling for land reform and democracy.

In 1647, having formulated his direct and simple approach to Christianity, Fox began to preach publicly. By 1651 he had a small band of travelling preachers, but they often met a harsh reception. Preaching against social injustice and the established church and using non-violent civil disobedience brought them into regular conflict with authority. Fox was imprisoned on many occasions.

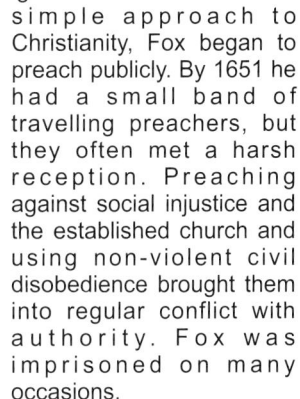

George Fox

In 1652 Fox set off for Sedbergh. There he preached to over 1000 people, mostly Westmorland **Seekers**, on nearby Firbank Fell. This is generally taken as the point at which the Quakers, or Friends, were established. A **Permanent Meeting** was set up by Fox at Brigflatts and the meeting house built there is still in use today.

Fox was arrested in 1655 and taken to Oliver Cromwell. The meeting went well with Fox "*speaking truth to power*", but although Fox met Cromwell several more times, persecution of the Quakers continued. In 1657 it is estimated that 1000 Quakers were in prison.

Fox went on to travel the world spreading his message. When he died in 1691 it is estimated he had 50,000 followers.

The Quakers, though, have had an impact on social affairs quite out of proportion to their numbers and their influence on campaigners for social justice resounds to this day.

The western Howgills from the south (above). The climb up Settlebeck Gill (below).

Approaching the ridge climb to Calders.

GEOLOGY: *Coniston Grit* makes up most of the bedrock underfoot as you cross the Howgills. A hard tough **greywacke** that gives generally firm dry walking, it stretches in a band across southern Lakeland to the sea. Hard mudstones and siltstones known as **Bannisdale Slate** form much of the south and north western parts of the Howgills, but only a thin section is crossed unseen at the northern end of the track as you drop to the hamlet of Bowderdale. Thin mudstone beds outcrop occasionally along the path, showing as short bluish bands of sharp laminations or ridges. Beds of finer sandstone underlie the start of the climb up Settlebeck Gill and the mound of Hazelgill Knott in the north.

The ancient rocks of the Howgill Fells were laid down over 400 million years ago, during the Silurian period. At that time the Dales landmass lay near the South Pole, under the Iapetus Ocean. Sand and mud were deposited on the ocean floor, then buried and compressed between colliding tectonic plates. The heat and pressure caused a partial metamorphosis of the rocks, turning the sandstone into tough greywacke and the mudstone into poor quality slate. Then, towards the end of the Carboniferous Period, around 290 million years ago, these ancient rocks were uplifted west of the Dent Fault to form the Lakeland and Howgill Fells.

These hard, dense rocks have proved resistant to erosion from weather and ice, leaving the distinctive rounded hills of the Howgills.

Looking south from West Fell, up Langdale Beck to the Calf on the left.

21. The Calf to West Fell *[3.4 miles]*

1.   From the Calf set off along the main path heading north east.

2.   The track swings gently to the right and eventually the head of a deep valley opens on the left, with a very faint track heading off above it. Ignore this and continue until you pass a small tarn on your left, which may dry out completely in summer.

The obvious track continues straight on here, beginning to drop and swing left. This is the old drove route down into Bowderdale and is a safe, sheltered alternative way off the tops if the weather deteriorates. The path continues along the left side of the dale, above the beck to the right, for several quiet, lonely miles before rising eventually to the left to pass above a wall on the right and join the main ridge route as it drops down from West Fell.

3.   Otherwise, the ridge route cuts off left on a faint track immediately after passing the small tarn. At first the view is hidden by the hill brow, but as you cross, the way ahead becomes clear. The long ridge route stretches out with the first peak of Hazelgill Knott prominent. To the left is the deep valley of Langdale and to the right the long deep valley of Bowderdale. Because the terrain in each direction is so similar, the only danger here is to set out too far to the left and find yourself descending **the Grains** into Langdale, but in clear weather this is obvious and with a little care should not be a problem.

4.   As you descend the first hill towards Hazelgill Knott the view ahead is excellent. *Although the route over the Howgills so far may have been busy, these northern fells are seldom visited and the sense of isolation soon becomes apparent. You are unlikely to meet many others as you cross this ridge and, for the next four miles, the only company may be skylarks and curlews.*

Looking north from around the Calf

5.   The track ahead is easy to follow, but wet in places. It seems you have left the limestone country behind and are once again crossing peaty grit underfoot.

6.   The top of Hazelgill Knott is soon reached. *There are more excellent views from here, particularly back up to Bowderdale Head where Cautley Crag can be seen, and down to the left along the snaking route of Langdale Beck. Ahead the line of the Orton Fells can be seen below the towering Pennine range in the distance.*

7.   After a long, easy, quiet trek, you finally reach West Fell - the last ridge peak. *Once again the views back up towards the Calf are excellent, with the peak of Ingleborough showing in the distance between Cautley Crags and Yarlside.*

22. West Fell to Newbiggin-on-Lune [3.9 miles]

1. As you reach the northern slopes of West Fell it is well worth pausing to investigate the excellent views ahead. *To the left, several northern Howgill ridges lead to the more distant Lakeland Fells. From the right, the Pennine range arcs in and across, with Cross Fell prominent in the distance directly ahead. Below and nearer, the humble Orton Fells stretch like a wall to link the two mountain ranges. Ahead, Sunbiggin Tarn can be clearly seen and behind it Great Kinmond, with its limestone scars glinting in the sun. Left of this is Great Asby Scar. Over to the right, beyond the deep Potts Valley is Crosby Garrett Fell. Immediately below, Bowderdale Beck meanders towards the tiny hamlet of Bowderdale.* It is an easy, steady descent from here.

2. As you descend, swing right to join an intake wall on the right and follow this down to a gate. The track then drops above a wooded area to another gate in a field above a crumbling barn.

3. Through the gate the track now follows the wall on the left, eventually joining a lane which leads on the right into Bowderdale itself.

4. This quiet farm lane crosses Bowderdale Beck at a delightful small stone bridge, which is a nice spot for a break. The lane then swings to pass under the A685 before climbing to join the original Tebay-Kirkby Stephen road below Rigg End farm.

Here a shortcut is possible for those not wishing to enter Newbiggin-on-Lune. Take the farm lane up past Rigg End farmhouse and through the gate. Although no right of way exists, this is Open Access Land. Follow the deeply rutted tracks up beside the left wall and turn sharp left at the wall top to head up to the hill ridge. Here the tracks become unclear in places, but the route heads across the open moor in a north easterly direction, finally joining the main path from Newbiggin-on-Lune on to Tarn Moor.

5. Otherwise, follow the quiet road right for a further mile to cross the busy A685 into Newbiggin-on-Lune.

ENCLOSURES: The Howgills are unusual in that there are no walls on the open fells. The miles of dry stone walls that cross most of the Dales are the result of the Enclosure Acts that parcelled the land, particularly after 1750.

Before this much of the upland areas were open pasture held in common, with grazing rights managed by manorial courts.

After the civil war more landowners began to fence off common land, either forcefully or by individual Acts of Parliament. A series of General Enclosure Acts in 1836, 1840 and 1845 made it possible for them to enclose land without reference to Parliament. Over a fifth of England was enclosed by this process. Although undoubtedly land was improved as a result, the main beneficiaries were the already established landowners, the losers the tenant farmers and labourers.

"The law locks up the man or woman, who steals the goose from off the common; but lets the greater villain loose, who steals the common from the goose."

FELL PONIES: With a bit of luck you'll catch sight of the famous Fell ponies when you're crossing the Howgills. To see them galloping across the open fellside with their long tails streaming behind them is a moment to be treasured.

Fell ponies are a native English breed best seen running wild on the Cumbrian fells. A handful of local farms hold the rights to graze the 70 or so seen today on the Howgills. Traditionally reared Fell ponies remain outside all year round. The mares form small groups of five or six that roam the hills together, but the stallions are kept down on the farm. Each spring the mares are rounded up and brought down for breeding, released again after a few weeks to fend for themselves. It is thought that this hard life helps to give Fell ponies their tough, alert character.

The ponies, with their distinctive shaggy, untrimmed manes and tails, are descended from animals that first crossed from the continent at the end of the last ice age. The early Fell pony made an ideal working animal - strong, sure footed and big enough for a grown man to ride, but not so big that loading and unloading were difficult. Once widely used to transport wool, slate and ore, today they are very popular as family ponies and are often used in riding stables and trekking centres because of their steady temperaments and useful size.

Breeders on the Howgills currently face the same problems as all hill farmers. It would be a tragedy if the day ever came when ponies are no longer to be seen roaming wild across the fells. Enjoy them while you can.

Fell ponies (above and opposite). Not all ponies on the fell are Fell ponies (below).

Alternative bad weather route from Sedbergh to Newbiggin-on-Lune via Cautley and Ravenstonedale.

This alternative route follows the river Rawthey along the eastern foot of the Howgills to Cautley, then follows Wandale Beck to cross the pass between Wandale Hill and Harter Fell before dropping into Ravenstonedale. A further mile of road walking brings you into Newbiggin-on-Lune. This is a fine and interesting alternative route.

20. (Alternative section) Sedbergh to Straight Bridge *[1.3 miles]*

From the town centre, head back down to New Bridge which crosses the river Rawthey. Just before crossing, steps lead down on the left to the river. A lovely gentle walk along the riverside now follows, over a few stiles, until the road crosses the river at Straight Bridge. Climb the steps up to the road and cross with great care, before passing through a stile opposite to rejoin the riverside.

20B. Alternative route from Straight Bridge to Cross Keys, Cautley *[3.4 miles]*

After crossing a further stile, the way rises away from the riverside before dropping to the farm house at Buckbank. Pass through several gates to the right of a cowshed and, with the farmhouse on the right, pass out onto the quiet road.

Turning right, follow the road as it drops down between trees to Ellerthwaite, before rising again high above the river which runs down to the right, to pass through a couple of gates by Thursgill Farm. The track, now rougher, drops again to cross Hoblake Beck at a gated bridge before climbing again to Fawcett Bank. Pass the house on the left, swinging back to continue through a gate with the sunken track rising alongside a fence on the left. The route is easy to follow as it shadows the river below on the right along the valley. Crossing through a gate to continue with the fence on the right, there are splendid views across to Baugh Fell beyond on the right, with the two hills of Wandale Hill and Harter Fell awaiting ahead. Eventually pass through a gate to continue with the fence on the right. Dramatic views of Cautley Crag and the Spout come into view on the left, as you drop to pass through the right gate of two ahead. Go beyond the wall corner on the left to a footbridge across Cautley Home Beck. Swinging right, head away from the crags and follow the river on the right to another footbridge which takes you over the river to the Cross Keys Temperance Inn.

21B. Cross Keys to Gais Gill *[3.1 miles]*

Return across the footbridge at Cross Keys and turn right at a fork in the track to climb above the side of Backside Beck. The track levels out before dropping to a ford across the beck to reach Narthwaite. However, the crossing can be difficult, especially after heavy rain, so be prepared for wet feet! A footbridge marked on the OS map further downstream no longer exists. Through the gate, climb the track up to the farm. Go into the farmyard and turn left just beyond a barn, through another gate, to rise with the bridleway as it follows the wall on the right. Ignore the other obvious tracks on the left to

Cross Keys Inn

keep with the sunken bridleway as it continues upwards.

The wall on the right all but disappears beneath a sparse hedgerow but the track, though rough and muddy, is unmistakeable. It soon becomes easier to follow the bridleway over to its right as it climbs higher, revealing a magnificent view of the road below swinging away, with Wild Boar Fell beyond. Harter Fell directly ahead dominates.

As it passes a couple of ruins at Wandale, the track opens out into a nice, broad green way and soon drops to the farm at Adamthwaite. Pass to the right of the farm and up onto the tarmac road which swings away to the right as it climbs again beside Little Harter Fell. There is a great feeling of isolation here. The high point is reached at Cross and the views ahead open out, before being lost again as the road drops to cross Gais Gill Beck at a bridge.

22B. Gais Gill to Ravenstonedale and Newbiggin-on-Lune *[3.7 miles]*

After crossing the bridge the road rises and the open views ahead return. The lovely village of Ravenstonedale appears, with Crosby Garrett Fell beyond and the southern foothills of the Howgills spread out to the left.

Ravenstonedale is soon reached, crossing a bridge on the right before dropping into the heart of the village from Town Head. There are pubs, B&Bs and a small shop here, so it's a good place to stay.

After turning left to pass the Black Swan Hotel and shop, continue above the church on the right to drop down to the Kings Head Hotel. Follow the road left until you reach the main A685. A cycle and walk way, opened in 2012, runs parallel to the busy trunk road on the left for quarter of a mile to join a quiet back road, bearing left into Newbiggin-on-Lune. This leads into the centre of the village.

The English Monks

The present building of St Oswald's Church in Ravenstonedale dates from the 18th century, but it is built on the site of a Gilbertine monastic house, remains of which can still be seen on the northern side of the church.

The Gilbertines were the only English monastic order, founded in 1131 by Gilbert of Sempringham, the son of a Norman knight and a Saxon mother. It was based on the Cistercian order, but had both nuns and monks sharing the same monastery. This would eventually lead to scandal with allegations of several nuns found "heavy with child"!

The monastic house at Ravenstonedale was small, with just eight cannons and a few lay brethren. There were probably no women here. Built around 1200 AD it was linked to the main Gilbertine monastery at Watton, East Yorkshire.

A wintery Sunbiggin Tarn (above). Castle Folds on Great Asby Scar with the northern Howgill Fells behind (below). (Both aerial photos © Simon Ledingham)

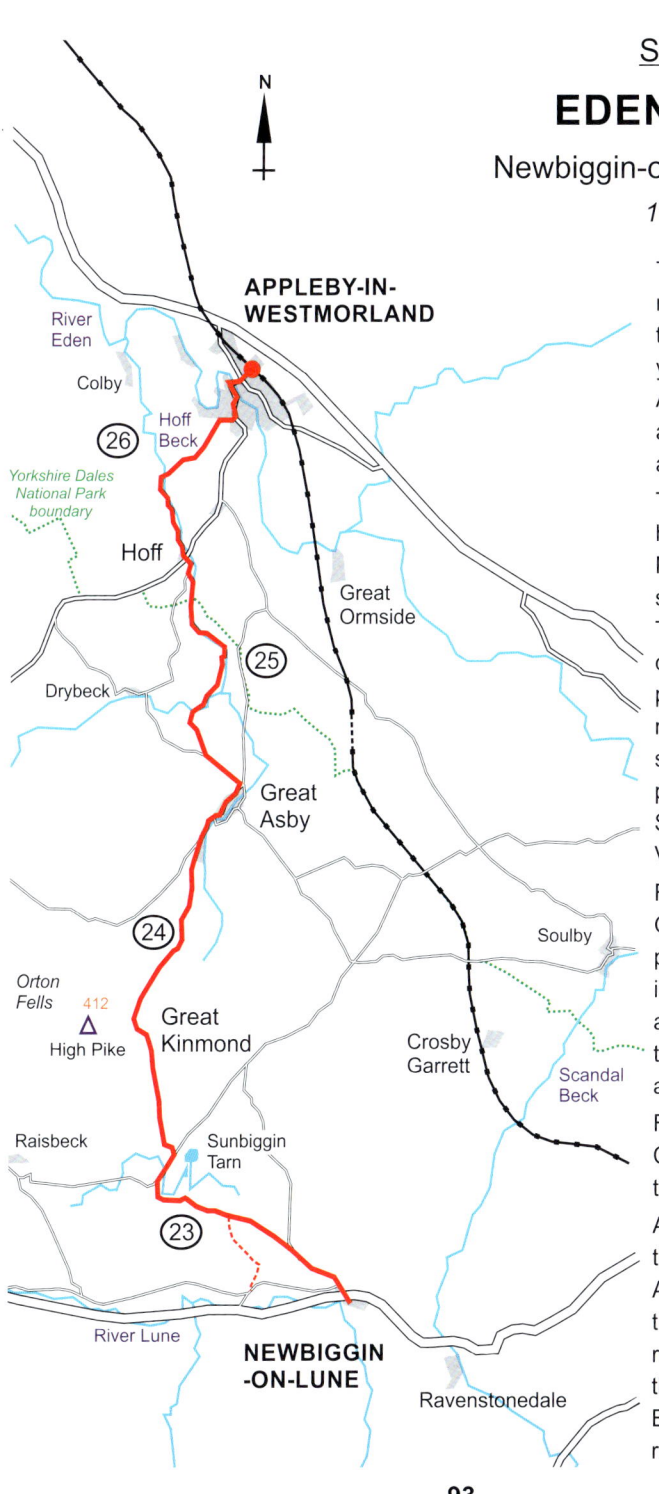

Section 6
EDEN VALLEY
Newbiggin-on-Lune to Appleby
12.7 miles

The final section has a relaxed, winding down feel to it as you head towards your destination at Appleby-in-Westmorland and the end of your adventure.

The day begins with a short hike over Ravenstonedale Moor to reach the isolated splendour of Sunbiggin Tarn. Then a surprise – a climb beside the humble peak of Great Kinmond reveals the vast and spectacular limestone pavement of Great Asby Scar. Ahead the lush Eden Valley beckons.

From the lovely village at Great Asby, the halfway point on this last leg, there is a gentle riverside ramble along Hoff Beck, passing the picturesque Rutter Mill and its delightful waterfall.

Finally the tower of Appleby Castle comes into view and the walking is almost over.

All that remains is to enjoy the old fashioned charm of Appleby before climbing the hill and making the return journey by train on the Settle to Carlisle Line - England's most beautiful railway.

23. Newbiggin-on-Lune to Great Kinmond *[3.7 miles]*

1. Leave Newbiggin-on-Lune and cross the busy A685 to climb the Great Asby Road for ¾ mile. The road passes High Lane farm and an electricity sub station. A number of tracks run off from the road across the grass towards the wall on the left as it falls away, but don't leave the road yet. Continue on awhile until a large, isolated stone barn appears on the right.

2. The path follows a right of way across Ravenstonedale Moor which was created in 2003 to cater for Coast to Coast walkers heading in the opposite direction. Although this area is now **Open Access Land** it is easier to locate and follow the path. Unfortunately, there is just a small waymark post at this end and the start of the path near Brackenber is unclear. Just past the lone stone barn the path can be picked up as a faint track about 20 metres from the road and running parallel to it. The track begins to swing gently away from the road to head north west over the grassland and as you cross an access lane to Gracetemoor the path ahead becomes clearer.

3. Eventually the path passes a walled enclosure on the right to reach the brow of the hill and the way ahead is now clear. *There are fine views of the Lakeland Fells in the distance, as well as the Howgills to the left and the humbler Orton Fells to the right.*

4. The path eventually drops to a wall corner, where a footbridge crosses a muddy beck and leads to a gate. Through this the path swings left and rises through heather, curving gently back to the right. *Sunbiggin Tarn now makes a fine sight to the right, with the modest peak of Great Kinmond to its left.*

5. Below to the right, Tarn Sike beck runs around a domed island. The path follows the line of the beck and swings right to head out onto the quiet Orton Rd.

6. Join the road and follow it north east for a quarter of a mile.

7. Eventually, just before the tarn, a public bridleway sign points off to the left. *This too is part of the modern Coast to Coast route.* There are a number of tracks, but the main broad track is fairly clear as it heads away, curving left after a while before swinging right again to climb gently northwards. At a crossing of tracks, the route leaves the Coast to Coast path, which turns left. Instead continue straight on, through scattered twisted hawthorn trees, to reach a gate. Through the gate, follow the wall on the left as it continues to climb.

24. Great Kinmond to Great Asby *[3.1 miles]*

1. Another gate in a fence leads back onto Open Access Land. *Here the cairn up to the right on Great Kinmond is tempting, but it is well short of the peak.* The way continues straight on alongside the wall, through increasing outcrops of limestone, to finally reach another gate in a wall which crosses ahead.

2. Through the gate a path crosses from right to left.

Ahead a cairn is visible and a short excursion to it is recommended. Cross the rough limestone pavement with care to reach it. The near panoramic views are excellent. Across to the left, the wide limestone terraces of Great Asby Scar lead away to the distant Lakeland Fells. These are the finest limestone pavements in the north of England outside the Ingleborough/Malham area. Ahead the view of the Pennine range rising above the Eden Valley is magnificent and will remain with you all the way down to Great Asby. Looking back, the long, lonely entrance to Bowderdale is still clear as it leads back into the Howgills.

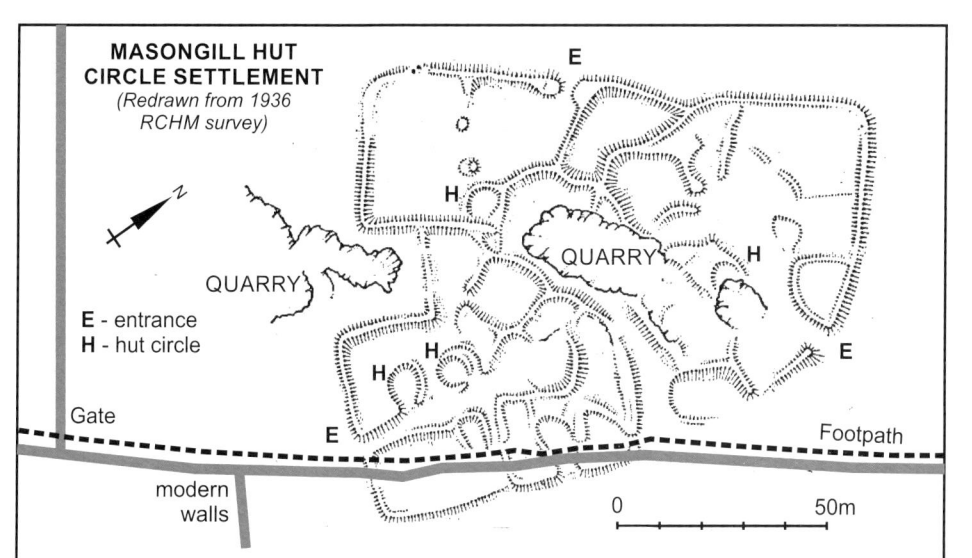

MASONGILL HUT CIRCLE SETTLEMENT
(Redrawn from 1936 RCHM survey)

E - entrance
H - hut circle

The ancient village settlement near Muddy Gill Farm consists of an irregular enclosure with internal subdivisions containing shaped stock pens and huts. The enclosure wall is of turf-covered limestone rubble and earth up to 4.5m wide and 1.5m high. It dates from the period of the Roman occupation and is classified as **Romano-British**, although the settlement was certainly that of native Celts and would have been almost identical to those built in the Iron Age before the Romans arrived. There is damage in the centre of the site caused by later quarrying. Now a Scheduled Ancient Monument, the path passes right through it.

3. Return to the gate to pick up the path as it swings away to the left to a wall corner. Just past the wall corner and before a more prominent track ahead, the path takes a sharp 90 degree right turn to drop down to a fence. There is a waymarked gate in the fence but this should be ignored and the fence followed instead down to the right.

4. Ignoring the more obvious track which pulls away to the right, stick close to the fence on your left until you reach a gate in a wall corner.

5. Through the gate, follow the wall on your right, heading straight towards the Pennines ahead, through two more gates. *In the next field the bumps and ruts in the floor mark the earthworks of an ancient Celtic settlement that once existed here **(see box)**.*

6. At the bottom of this field the lane from Masongill farm crosses and leads out to the left onto the Great Asby road. Turn right to cross the cattle grid and pass through a small wall stile immediately on the left.

7. The wall on the left is now followed through several stiles and gates to reach a stile beside a walled track. Through the stile, cross the field ahead to join another wall on the left and continue with this through several gates to reach Clockeld farm.

8. This is a busy working farm. Drop straight down through it, passing the farmhouse on your right, through several gates and follow the farm drive out onto a quiet walled lane.

9. The lane now leads down into the small village of Great Asby.

Don't be too surprised to hear the distant thunder of artillery, as not far away is the military camp and testing range at Warcop.

WILDLIFE: From the open moorland around Sunbiggin Tarn and the last climb over limestone pavement at Great Asby Scar to the lanes, riverbank and woodland of the Eden Valley, the final section of the walk offers a variety of contrasting habitats.

Sunbiggin Tarn is a site of Special Scientific Interest, recognised for its importance to a number of species. Until 1998 a colony of 10,000 **Black Headed Gull** nested there. The mystery of their sudden disappearance has never been explained. Smaller numbers still breed at the tarn along with **Snipe**, **Water Rail** and **Tufted Duck**. **Teal**, **Little Grebe**, **Great Crested Grebe**, **Goldeneye** and **Mallard** can also be seen.

Along the lane approaching Hoff the hedgerow is dominated by **Wild Gooseberry** and hidden amongst the **Lords and Ladies** on Colby Lane is the inconspicuous but charming **Moschatel**, also known as **Town Hall Clock** because 4 of its 5 faces look out at right angles.

Swallow and **Common Sandpiper** can be seen along Hoff Beck and **Sand Martin** nest in holes in the sandy banks of the river.

Red Squirrel live in the conifer and broadleaved woodland near Rutter Mill. Wooded areas in the north of England are now one of the few places they survive in Britain and Cumbria Wildlife Trust encourages people to report their sitings to help confirm their distribution.

Some of the woodlands in the area were once coppiced, the trees being felled to ground level to harvest the timber. The trees re-grow numerous stems forming a distinctive landscape. Woodlands were divided into areas called coups and these were coppiced in rotation every ten to fifteen years depending on the desired product (bobbins, fencing, charcoal etc.). This management technique is valuable for wildlife as it creates a variety of age structures in the woodland encouraging ground flora, butterflies, and nesting birds. You will walk through a small area of coppice just before Bandley Bridge, which supports spring flowers such as **Wood Anemone**, **Wood Sorrel**, **Primrose** and **Wild Strawberry**.

Background photo: Coppiced woods near Bandley Bridge.

(1) Wild Strawberry (N.E.W.)   *(2) Primrose (N.E.W.)*
(3) Wood Anemone (N.E.W.)   *(4) Sand Martin (N.E.W.)*

(5) Red Squirrel (N.E.W.)   *(6) Common Sandpiper (N.E.W.)*
(7) Great Crested Grebe (N.E.W.)   *(8) A Swallow feeds its young (N.E.W.)*

25. Great Asby to Hoff *[3.5 miles]*

1. Follow the road through Great Asby passing the prominent double bell tower of St Peter's Church on your right. The road swings in towards the beck on the right, before curving left to leave the village and rise away above it.

2. At a crossroads by a cemetery turn left to climb the quiet road towards **Drybeck**.

3. The road soon levels out, providing good views of the Pennines once again to the right. Just as the road begins to drop, a lane marked to **Hayton Holme** leads to the right.

4. Ignoring the turn off to the right halfway down the lane, continue to drop down to a cluster of farm buildings at Howe Slacks. Pass below the buildings to turn right, with the beck on your left, and cross to a gateway on the left. A narrow track now follows the beck to a stile at the end on the right.

5. Once over the stile, head diagonally across the field to a gated footbridge.

6. Over the bridge turn right and head across towards the far wall. Look for the stile in the wall to the right of the gate.

7. The path continues across two further fields and a stile, following the course of the beck on the right. The fields can be muddy in places after rain. Eventually a gate up on the left field corner leads to a clearing above Rutter Force, which can be viewed from the fence on the right. Cross a stile to drop behind the mill buildings to a gate onto a road.

8. Turn right and walk down to view the attractive waterfall, mill and waterwheel from the footbridge over Hoff Beck. *This is a great spot for a picnic.*

9. Turn back up the road a few yards to the gate where you joined it. Opposite is a gateway marked **Footpath to Hoff**. Cross to a stile to rejoin Hoff Beck on your right.

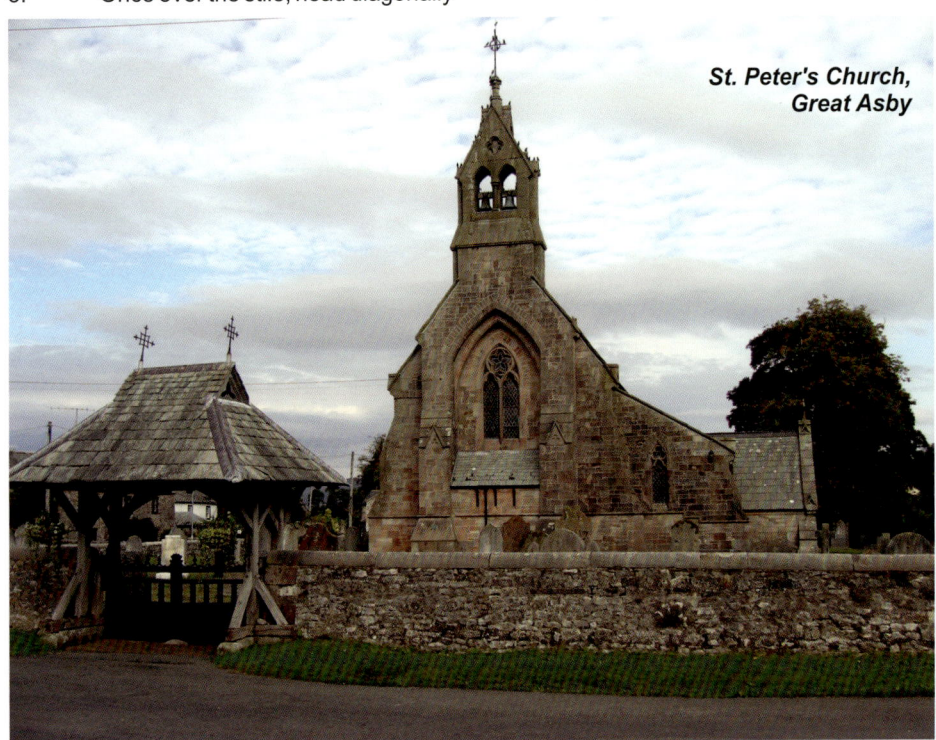

St. Peter's Church, Great Asby

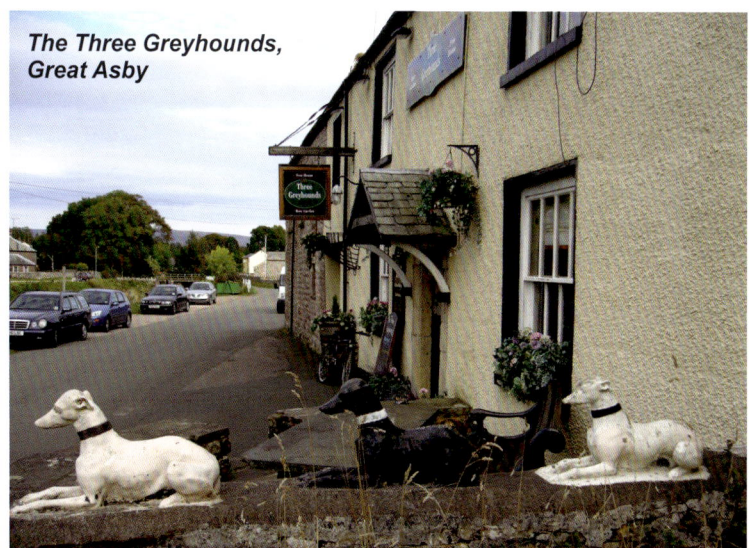

The Three Greyhounds, Great Asby

which the path drops back down to the right to a gate. The beck is rejoined in a small meadow which leads to a gate at **Bandley Bridge**.

4. Cross the bridge to rise to a stile and just ahead cross another stile in the wall on the right. The path now rises away from the wall to climb the field to a stile in the wall ahead.

5. The view ahead now opens out, to reveal Appleby Castle poking above the trees against a backdrop of the pyramid of Murton Pike, the deep ravine of High Cup Nick and the line of the North Pennine Fells. Your walk is nearly at an end.

6. The path continues diagonally over the next field to a stile in the right hand wall. Now continue to the left and follow the wall to another stile at a sharp bend in a narrow enclosed way. A gate opposite leads straight on down to join **Colby Lane**. On the lane turn right and go on to join Scattergate below the castle walls.

7. Cross the road and turn left to follow the castle wall on your right as it begins to climb to the narrow **Shaws Wiend** and enter Appleby at the top of **Boroughgate** by the High Cross. The entrance gates to the castle are on your right (*castle tours can be booked at the Tourist Information Centre*).

Head down Boroughgate into the heart of the town where a number of pubs and a well earned pint await.

10. Soon cross a stile to a footbridge. Cross the beck and continue downstream with the beck now on your left.

11. After three further stiles cross a farmtrack leading from a large bridge on your left, to climb a further stile just ahead.

12. Continue with the beck still on your left through a farmgate to a footbridge. Cross this and swing right to a gate, leading to a narrow track which takes you out onto a lane. A right turn brings you onto the road at Hoff.

26. Hoff to Appleby *[2.4 miles]*

1. With Hoff Bridge on your right, cross straight over the road and up the farm lane. Fork right at Stonekirk House and pass through a gate into a yard. Another gate in the wall on the right leads into a small field. Cross this to a stile and rejoin the beck on your right.

2. Continue with the beck on your right to cross four more fields and two more stiles before reaching a large wooded copse on your left. Another stile leads down to **Cuddling Hole**, a lovely spot at the water's edge opposite a crag wall.

3. The path now follows a short steep climb up the wooded bank to a stile, over

(Above) Hoff Beck. (Below) Rutter Force and Rutter Mill.

GEOLOGY: As you drop from the limestone pavements of Great Asby Scar, the characteristic red sandstone of the Eden Valley first shows itself in the buildings of Great Asby and beyond.

The limestone dips beneath the younger sandstone beds somewhere around Hoff, but here the bedrock is hidden beneath rich glacial and alluvial deposits that give the valley its lush appearance.

The wall and window edgings of the Kingdom Hall in Appleby reflect the sandstone outcrop on which it's built.

The red sandstones are the youngest rocks in the region, laid down when Britain was part of a large tropical desert, around 270 million years ago. The Penrith sandstone appears to have been formed from wind-blown desert dunes in the Permian period, whilst the Sherwood (*or St. Bees*) sandstone to the east was deposited by water, probably in flash floods, during the later Triassic. This was the time of the Permian-Triassic mass extinction event when around 90% of all earth's species disappeared and led eventually to the rise of the dinosaurs in the mid to late Triassic.

The red sandstone colours the banks of Hoff Beck and in Appleby outcrops are exposed alongside the road leading from the Sands to Bongate.

The final approach to Appleby.

APPLEBY-IN-WESTMORLAND

The small market town of Appleby is the historic county seat of Westmorland.

On April 1st 1974, at the stroke of a pen, the county of Westmorland disappeared altogether from the administrative map of England. Parliament's latest design for local government redrew traditional county boundaries which had existed for 800 years or more. Westmorland now fell under the control of the new Cumbria County Council, as did areas of the West Riding of Yorkshire such as Dent, Sedbergh and Garsdale. In response the parish councillors of Appleby changed the town's name to **Appleby-in-Westmorland**, to keep the ancient link.

The earliest known settlement was Danish, based in the area of Bongate, or Old Appleby. A **hog-back** tombstone, built into the wall of St. Michael's Church, dates from this period.

By the time of the Norman conquest, the Eden Valley was under Scottish control. In 1092 King William Rufus pushed the Scots back beyond Carlisle and the first castle at Appleby was built. A new settlement was established inside the river loop, under the castle's protection, and a bridge built to link the new town with the old. The basic layout of the town has changed little since then.

By 1135 Appleby was under Scottish rule once more. Indeed the town changed hands several times over the next 250 years, often with great bloodshed. In between however, the town prospered. In 1200 King John granted the town a Charter and from then on it became independent from the castle.

The Scottish invasion in 1388 laid waste to the town. It remained desolate for over a century and a half. In a report to the Crown in 1515, officials record that they **"found the said borough or town of Appleby was greatly diminished and fallen into ruin…"**

Appleby never fully recovered from that time, though Lady Anne Clifford helped restore much of the town's fortunes.

Horses are washed in the River Eden

Today Appleby is an attractive, quiet rural town that retains an old fashioned charm. Its wide main street, Boroughgate, has been described as one of the finest in England.

In June each year the town is transformed with the arrival of the annual horse fair. In the weeks before, temporary encampments pop up along the routes into Appleby.

It began as a market for cattle, sheep and horses and has been held regularly since the late 1750s. By the early 20th century *Appleby New Fair* was very much the horse fair that we know today. It is not an organised event as such, just a traditional gathering of Romany and Irish families traveling to meet up with old friends, celebrate their culture and conduct business - particularly buying and selling horses. It is probably the biggest and oldest such gathering in Europe.

2013 saw over 5,000 Gypsies and Travellers gather, with another 10,000 daily visitors who came to enjoy the spectacle. All this in a town with a normal population of just 3,000.

Caravans gather around Fair Hill, the traditional site of the fair. Horses are washed in the river Eden and run on the **flashing lane** in front of potential buyers. They are paraded from Fair Hill down along the Sands to Bongate, but they are not allowed across the bridge into the town itself. 1,500 may be sold over the six days of the fair.

There's a touch of the Wild West about the event and the anarchic atmosphere doesn't suit everyone's sensibilities. It provides, however, a rare glimpse of times long past when such events were common.

Lady Anne Clifford

It is impossible to explore Appleby without coming across the name of Lady Anne Clifford.

Anne was born at Skipton Castle in 1590, into the privilege and power of the land-owning aristocracy. She grew up in London and as a child was a favourite of Queen Elizabeth. Her two elder brothers died young and her father, George, chose to leave the family estates to his brother rather than his daughter.

When George died in 1605, Anne's mother Lady Margaret began a legal battle to regain the estates for Anne. After Lady Margaret died in 1616, Anne took up the fight herself.

When she was 19, Anne had married Richard Sackville, 3rd Earl of Dorset, who spent much of his time socialising and gambling. She was put under enormous pressure to renounce her claim, not least by her husband who was looking for the compensation that would result. She even openly defied King James on the matter, much to his anger, but despite the bullying she wouldn't be budged.

Almost 40 years were to pass before she regained her inheritance.

In the midst of the English Civil War, in 1643, Anne's cousin Henry Clifford died suddenly whilst defending Skipton Castle for the Royalists. He had no male heir so at last the estates came back to Anne. She couldn't get near them though - Skipton Castle was still under siege.

When the civil war ended, Lady Anne Clifford was able at last to tour her estates in Yorkshire and Westmorland. Barden Tower and Brough Castle were ruins. Pendragon Castle was a *"heap of stones"* and Brougham Castle at Penrith was derelict. Skipton Castle had been partially demolished on Cromwell's orders and Appleby was in a similar state.

Yet, as her 60th birthday approached, Lady Anne Clifford set about restoring them all.

This was to become her life's work and her major legacy to the region. Somehow she persuaded Cromwell to let her rebuild Skipton Castle. She also restored churches at Ninekirks, Brougham, Mallerstang, Barden and Appleby, as well as building the almshouses in Appleby. She was generous to the poor, but was an autocratic and ruthless landlord.

She would travel the hundred miles between Skipton and Penrith, crossing the rugged and exposed Pennine uplands, in a carriage strung between two horses, with her huge entourage in tow. Today walkers can follow her route on the long distance path called ***Lady Anne's Way***.

Lady Anne Clifford lived to be 86. She died at Brougham Castle in 1676 and was buried in St Lawrence's Church, at the foot of Boroughgate in Appleby. Today, many of those buildings she restored are in ruins again. But the castles at Skipton and Appleby remain intact, monuments to a Proud Northern Lady.

APPLEBY-IN-WESTMORLAND

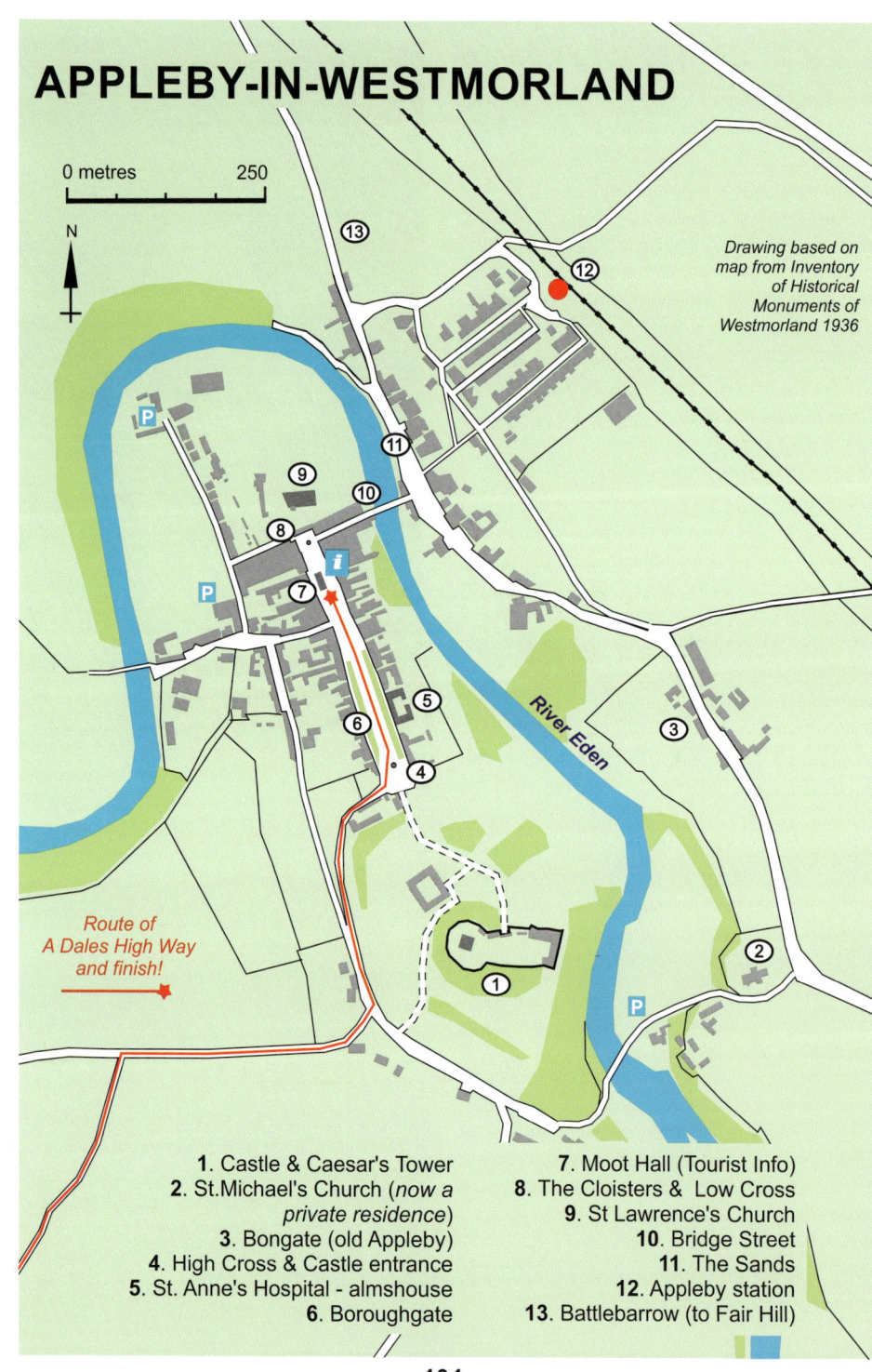

0 metres 250

Drawing based on map from Inventory of Historical Monuments of Westmorland 1936

Route of A Dales High Way and finish!

1. Castle & Caesar's Tower
2. St.Michael's Church (*now a private residence*)
3. Bongate (old Appleby)
4. High Cross & Castle entrance
5. St. Anne's Hospital - almshouse
6. Boroughgate
7. Moot Hall (Tourist Info)
8. The Cloisters & Low Cross
9. St Lawrence's Church
10. Bridge Street
11. The Sands
12. Appleby station
13. Battlebarrow (to Fair Hill)

Appleby Castle (Above) *(photo: © Simon Ledingham).* **High Cross (Below)**

THE SETTLE-CARLISLE RAILWAY

The 72-mile Settle to Carlisle Railway was the last great construction project of the Victorian era. It was built by navvies over some of the roughest, boggiest and most exposed terrain in England.

Yet there was no real intention to build it at all. When the Midland Railway company sought government approval for a new railway linking Settle to Carlisle, it was hoped that the plans alone would be enough to persuade rivals to share their western line more equitably. However, once the government granted approval, they insisted the project be completed.

Work began in 1869, with as many as 6,000 men working on the line at its peak. The navvies lived with their families in shanty towns along the route, places like Batty Wife Hole, Sebastopol, Inkerman, Jericho, Jerusalem and Tunnel Huts. Fourteen tunnels and 20 viaducts were constructed, but the cost was high. The tiny church at Chapel-le-Dale marks the burial spot of over 200 men, women and children who died through accident or disease building the line.

Ribblehead Viaduct is a quarter of a mile long with 24 arches. It stands 32 metres above the surrounding moorland on piers sunk through eight metres of peat and clay to the solid rock below. But even this miracle of Victorian engineering was marred by some shoddy workmanship. As early as 1934, for example, it was noticed that water was getting into the structure and causing damage. In 1989, when major repair work was finally undertaken, the cause was uncovered – a line of mysterious square holes in the original bitumen waterproof decking was letting water pour in. Evidently the bitumen layer was laid around the wooden scaffolding posts, which were subsequently sawn off at the surface. The waterproofing lasted only until the wooden stumps rotted away.

The line opened in 1876 and at its peak in 1920 carried 374,000 passengers. But three years later amalgamation between the rival private railway companies made the need for the line technically redundant. During the 1950s following nationalisation, many of the small stations and branch lines closed and although the main line survived the Beeching cuts of the 1960s, the writing was on the wall.

The battle for the Settle-Carlisle Line

By 1970 just two daily services were running, using old clapped-out diesels. Appleby was the only station open between Settle and Carlisle. The Ramblers ran a charter train in 1974 which was a huge sucess and led to a regular weekend DalesRail service financed by the National Park and local authorities.

In early 1981, however, British Rail made it clear that closure was inevitable, saying that

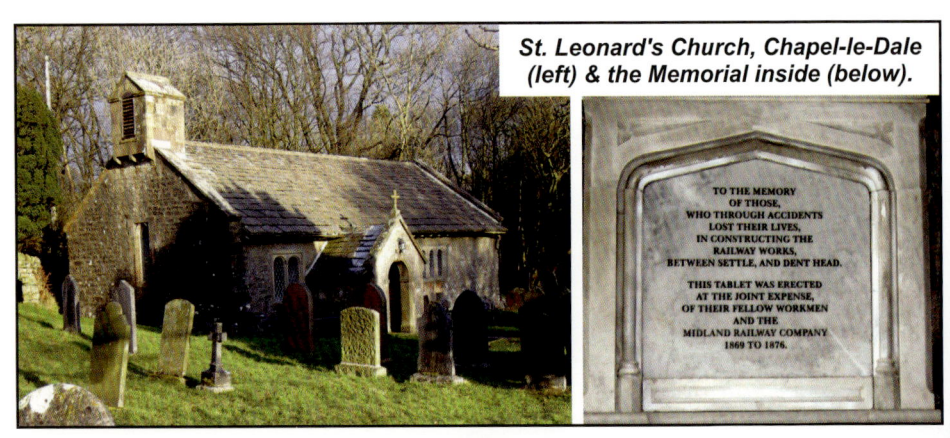

St. Leonard's Church, Chapel-le-Dale (left) & the Memorial inside (below).

the Ribblehead Viaduct was crumbling and would cost over £6 million to repair. The following June the inaugural meeting of the **Friends of the Settle-Carlisle Line** was held, at the instigation of Graham Nuttall, who became its first secretary. Graham was a modest Lancashire man who loved to walk the fells with his faithful companion Ruswarp (pronounced *Russup*). Ruswarp was later to gain fame as the only dog to become an official objector to the line closure.

Seasoned campaigners from organisations like Transport 2000 joined the impending battle and a Joint Action Committee was formed. In December 1983 the formal notice of closure was issued by BR. Thus began the longest running railway closure inquiry in British history. With a record number of objectors – 22,265 people and one dog - the battle was set to run for six years.

Meanwhile British Rail brought in Ron Cotton to oversee the line closure. Cotton took his job seriously and set about making the line as profitable as he could before it finally closed. Within three years he'd managed to double services, re-open eight stations and quadruple revenues! Much to his bosses embarrassment, Cotton proved that the line was commercially viable.

After a last-ditch attempt at privatisation, the government finally gave in and on April 11th 1989 announced the line's reprieve!

Loyal Ruswarp

The following year, on January 20th 1990, Graham Nuttall bought day return tickets from Burnley to Llandrindod Wells, to walk the Welsh mountains with his dog Ruswarp. When Graham didn't return his neighbours raised the alarm and police and mountain rescue teams went looking for him, but with no luck.

Eleven weeks later a lone walker found Graham's body by a mountain stream. Nearby was Ruswarp, who had loyally remained besides Graham throughout those long, cold winter months. The 14 year old border collie was so weak he had to be carried from the mountain, where he was cared for by Graham's aunt and uncle.

Ruswarp survived just long enough to attend Graham's funeral.

On April 11th, 2009, exactly 20 years after the Settle-Carlisle's official reprieve, a life-size bronze statue of Ruswarp was unveiled at the newly restored Garsdale Station, one of Graham's favourite spots: a fitting symbol of the heroic battle to save England's most beautiful railway line.

Graham Nuttall & Ruswarp
(photo © Sunday Mirror)

The Return Journey: Many people think that the Settle to Carlisle line is a heritage railway, running steam trains for tourists. In fact it is a main line rail route carrying passengers and freight between Carlisle and Leeds, with many daily services. Although steam charters run regularly at weekends through the summer, you're likely to be making the return journey on a speedy Diesel Sprinter. The journey is no less fascinating for that, so relax and enjoy the highlights of your walk from the comfort of the train.

(Opposite) After leaving Kirkby Stephen on the way to Garsdale, the train reaches the highest point at Ais Gill Summit, with Wild Boar Fell behind. *(photo © Pete Shaw)*
(Above) A frosty Ribblehead station. (Below) Settle station.

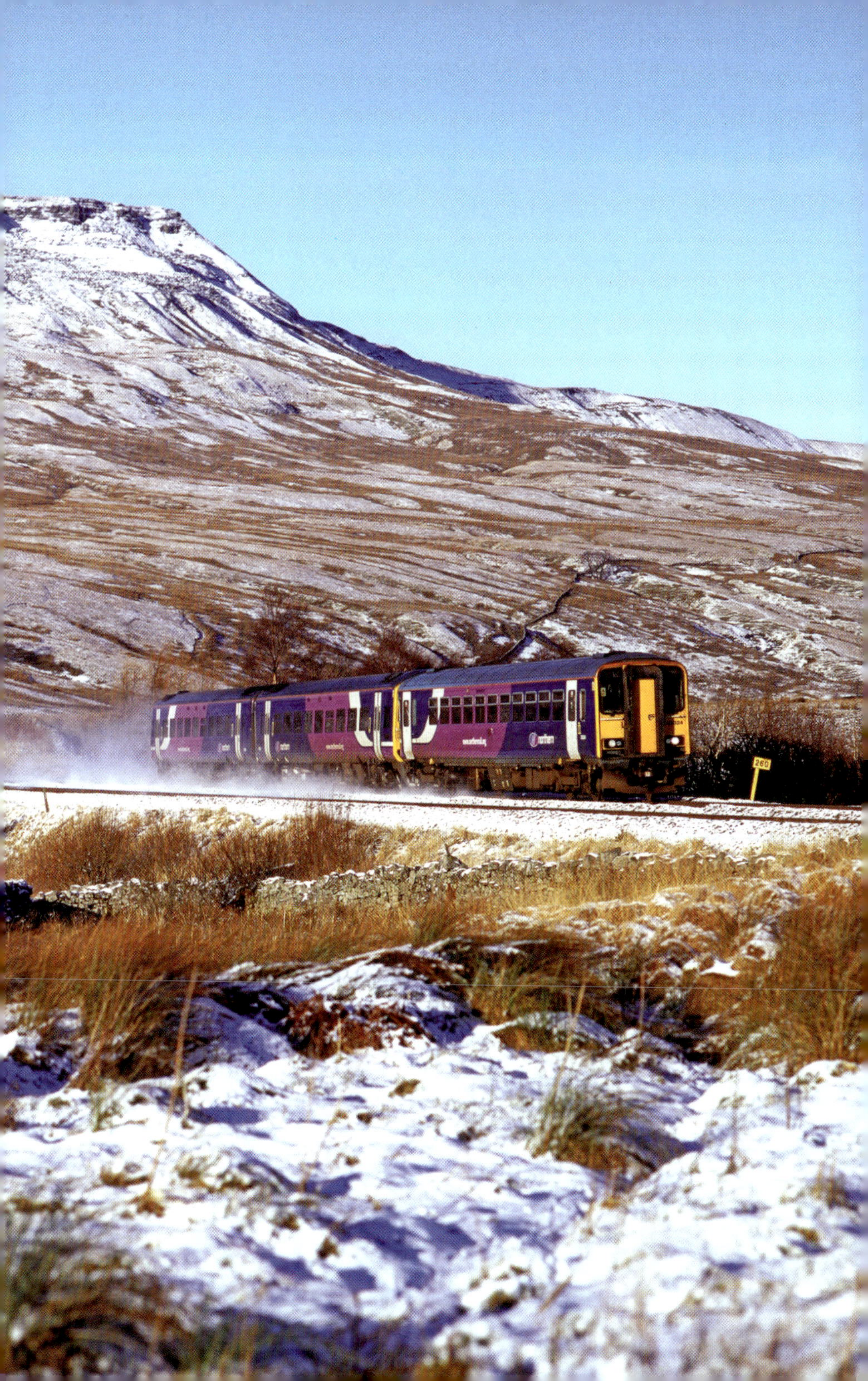
260

INDEX OF PLACES

*(Page numbers in **Bold Italics** indicate pictures)*

Adamthwaite 91
Addingham 4, 9, 10, 17, 23, 26, 30, 63
Addingham High Moor 17, **20**, 23, 25
Addingham Moorside 17, 23, 26
Aire river- 13, 17, 33, 34
Aire Gap 25, 31, 34
Ais Gill summit **109**
Albert Cave 47
All Saints Parish Church 21
Allotment the- 54
Alum Pot 55
Angel Inn 39
Appleby 4, 6, 7, 9, 10, 93, 99, **101**, 102, 103, 104, 106
Appleby Castle 10, 93, 99, 102, 103, 104, **105**
Arant Haw 82
Arten Gill 67
Attermire Cave 46, **47**
Attermire Scar *cover*, 46, **48**
Austwick 49
Austwick Beck 49, 51, 52

Backside Beck 90
Backstone Beck 22
Baildon 17
Baildon Moor 8, 17
Bandley Bridge **96**, 99
Barbondale 70, 77
Barden Moor 23, 30, 34, 42
Barden Tower 103
Barth Bridge 71, 77
Battlebarrow 104
Baugh Fell 67, 77, 81, 82, 90
Beamsley Beacon 23
Ben Rhydding 21
Bingley 4, 17, 22
Bingley Moor 17
Birch Close 19
Black Plantation 30
Black Swan Hotel 91
Blea Moor 65, 66, 67
Blea Moor Sidings 65, 66, 67
Bongate 102, 104

Boot of the Wold 67
Boroughgate 99, 102, 103, 104
Bowderdale 81, 85, 86, 87, 94
Bowderdale Beck 81, 87
Brackenber 94
Bradford 9, **14**, 15, 18, 19, 83
Braithwaite Wife Hole 62
Brigflatts 83
Bridge St. 104
Brough Castle 103
Brougham Castle 103
Bruntscar 65, 66, 75
Buckbank 90

Caesar's Tower 104
Calf the- 81, 82, **85**, **86**
Calders 82, **85**
Cam Fell 55, 62
Carlisle 6, 10, 46, 66, 106, 107, 108
Castle Folds **92**
Castleberg **46**
Castlehaw 10, **74**, 75, 82
Cautley 81, 90
Cautley Crag 86, 90
Cautley Home Beck 90
Cautley Spout 90
Celtic Wall the- 50
Chapel-le-Dale 4, 6, 7, 9, 49, 53, 54, 55, 62, 65, 66, 106
Chelker Reservoir 23, 27
Church Bridge 70
Clapham 49, 53, 54, 55
Clockeld 95
Clough river- 65, 77
Colby Ln 99
Colt Park 55, 62, 75
Cow Dub 79
Cowgill 77
Cracoe 39
Craven Fault 8, 9, **44**, 77
Craven Way 65, 67
Crook Farm 19
Crosby Garrett 93
Crosby Garrett Fell 87, 91
Cross Fell 87
Cross Keys 81, 90
Cross Keys Inn **90**
Crummack 51, 54

Crummack Dale 8, 49, 51, 52, 55, **56**
Cuddling Hole 99

Dee river- 65, 70
Deepdale 65, 66, 67, 70
Dent 4, 9, 65, 66, **69**, 70, **71**, **76**, 77, 78, 79, 102
Dent Fault 8, 9, 71, 77, 85
Dentdale 4, 6, 11, 65-79, **69**, **72**
Dobrudden 19, **24**, 25
Draughton Height 17, 26, **27**, 30
Dry Valley 43, 45, **48**
Drybeck 93, 98

Eden Valley 4, 6, 8, 9, 11, 93-105
Eden river- 93, **102**, 104
Eldwick 22
Eller Beck 66
Ellerbeck Gill 66
Ellerthwaite 90
Embsay Moor 34, 42

Fair Hill 102, 104
Fawcett Bank 90
Feizor 49, 50, 51
Fell Beck 53
Firbank Fell 83
Flasby 33, 34, 37
Flasby Beck **36**
Flasby Fell 10, 37, 42
Flasby Hall 37
Folly the- **10**, 46
Force Gill 67, **68**
Fountains Fell 42, 43, 44, 50
Frostrow 65, 74, 80, 82

Gais Gill 81, 90, 91
Gais Gill Beck 91
Gaping Gill **53**
Gargrave 4, 33, 35, 37, 75
Garsdale 4, 77, 102, 107
Gauber 10
Gawthrop **77**
Giggleswick 50
Glovershaw 19
Golcar 19, 22
Gordale Beck 33, 43
Gordale House 33, 42, 43
Gordale Ln **44**

Goredale Scar 33, 42, 44, **45**
Gracetemoor 94
Grains the- 86
Great Asby 4, 9, 93, 94, 95, **98**, **99**, 101
Great Asby Scar 11, 87, **92**, 93, 94, 96, 101
Great Coum 62, 65, 70
Great Douk Cave 62
Great Kinmond 87, 93, 94
Great Ormside 93
Great Shunner Fell 62
Great Whernside 42
Great Wold 67
Greensett 67
Greenside Beck 81
Grizedales 43

Harter Fell 81, 90, 91
Hawes 9
Hayton Holme 98
Hazelgill Knott 85, 86
Heber's Ghyll 23
Hellifield 4
Hetton 4, 9, 33, 39, 75
Hetton Common 39, 42
High Cross 10, 99, **105**
High Cup Nick 99
High Pike 93
Higher Bark House 51
Hill Inn 49, 55, 62, 65, 66
Hobdale Gill 82
Hoblake Beck 90
Hoff 93, 96, 98, 99, 101
Hoff Beck 93, 96, 98, **100**, 101
Hoff Bridge 99
Holebeck Gill 71, 74, 77
Hope Hill 18, 19, 22
Horton 4, 49, 55, 59, 63
Horncliffe 22
Howgills **1**, 4, 6, 7, 8, 11, 62, 70, 71, 74, 75, **80**, 81-91, **84**, **88**, **92**, 94
Howe Slacks 98
Humphrey Bottom 62
Hurtle Pot 66

Ilkley 4, 7, 9, 10, 17, 21, 22, 27, 63
Ilkley Crags 22
Ilkley Moor 17, 21, 34, 42
Ingleborough 4, **6**, 7, 11, 42, 46, 49-64, **57**, **60**, 65, 66, 67

110

Ingleborough Cave 53
Ingleborough Hillfort 10, **58**-59, 62
Ivescar 66, 75

Janet's Foss 33, 43
Jubilee Cave 46, 47

Keighley 4, 17, 19
Kings Head Hotel 91
Kingsdale Beck 65
Kirkby Fell 33, 42, 43, 46
Kirkby Lonsdale 77
Kirkby Stephen 4, 9, 77
Knoutberry Hill 67

Langcliffe 47
Langcliffe Weir 60
Langdale 86
Langdale Beck 81, **85**, 86
Langscar 43
Langscar Gate 43
Lanshaw Lad **22**
Leeds-Liverpool Canal 13, 17, **18**, 33
Little Harter Fell 91
Little Ingleborough 53
Little London 22
Long Lane 54
Long Preston 4
Longstone Fell 65, 71, 74, 77
Low Cross 104
Lunds 71
Lune river- 81, 93

Malham 4, 7, 8, 9, 33, **42**, 75
Malham Cove **32**, 33, 40, 43, **45**, **48**
Malham Rakes 44
Malham Tarn 33, 43, 44
Malhamdale 4, 6, 8, 33-48, 75
Mallerstang Edge 62
Manningham Mills 15, 19
Manor House 10, **21**, **23**
Masongill 10, **95**
Menwith Hill 22
Middleton Fell 65, 70, **77**, 82
Moor Lane Addingham 26, **27**
Moor Lane Hetton 33, **36**, 38, 42
Moot Hall 10, 104
Moughton 49, 52
Moughton Scar 51

Muddy Gill 95
Murton Pike 99

Nappa Cross 43
Nappa Gate 44
Narthwaite 90
New Bridge 74, 90
New Mill **12**, 13, 15
Newbiggin-on-Lune 4, 7, 9, 81, 87, 90, 91, 93, 94
Norber **52**

Old Hill Inn (*see* Hill Inn)
Orton Fells 81, 86, 87, 93, 94
Otley Chevin 19
Ovenden Moor 19

Park Fell 49, 54, 55, 62, 63
Pendle Hill 34, 42
Pendragon Castle 103
Pennythorne Hill 19
Pen-y-ghent 43, 49, 50, 51, 54, 55, 59, 67, 70
Piper's Crag 23, **24**, 25
Potts Valley 87

Randygill Top 81
Ravenstonedale 10, 81, 90, 91, 93
Ravenstonedale Moor 93, 94
Rawthey river- 65, 81, 90
Rawthey Bridge 77
Ray Gill 42
Ribble river- 46, 49, 50, **56**, 60
Ribblehead 4, 7, 9, 10, 49, 54, 55, 60, 62, 63, 65, 75, **108**
Ribblehead Viaduct 10, **64**, 65, 66, 106, **107**
Rigg End 67, 87
Rise Hill 65, 67, 70
Roberts Park 13, **15**
Rombalds Moor 4, 6, 10, 11, **16**, 17-32, **28**
Rombalds Way 25
Rough Haw 10, 34, **36**, **38**
Rutter Force 98, **100**
Rutter Mill 93, 96, **100**
Rye Loaf Hill 46
Rylstone 33, 34, 39

Saltaire 4, 6, 7, 9, 10, **12**, 13-15, 17, 18, 22

Salts Mill 10, 13, **16**, 18
Sands the- 102, 104
Scandal Beck 81
Scattergate 99
Sedbergh 4, 7, 9, 10, 63, 65, **74**, 75, 77, 81, **82**, 83, 90, 102
Selside 49, 55
Settle 4, 6, 9, **10**, 33, 43, 44, 46, 47, 49, 50, 60, 63, 106, 107, **108**
Settlebeck Gill 81, 82, **84**, 85
Sharp Haw 30, 33, **34**, **36**, 38
Shaws Wiend 99
Shipley 4, 14, 17, 63
Shipley Glen 18, **20**, **24**, 25
Simon Fell 49, **54**, 55, 62
Simon's Seat 42
Skipton 4, 7, 9, 10, 17, 27, **30**, 31, 33, 34, 35, 37, 39, 42, 63, 83
Skipton Castle 10, **30**, **31**, 34, 83, 103
Skipton Moor 17, 23, 25, **27**, 30, 34
Sleights Rd. 62
Small Banks 26
Smearset Scar 49, 50, 51
Souther Scales 49, 60, 62, **64**
Spicey Gill 22, 23
St. Andrew's Church 70, **71**
St. Anne's Hospital 10, 104
St. Lawrence's Church 103, 104
St. Leonard's Church 65, 66, **106**
St. Michael's Church 102, 104
St. Oswald's Church 10, **91**
St. Peter's Church **26**, **98**
Stackhouse 49, 50
Stainforth 4, 7, 9, 49, 50
Stainforth Bridge 50
Stainforth Force 49, **50**, 60
Station Inn 55, 62
Straight Bridge 81, 90
Street Farm 26
Stockdale Beck 43
Stockdale Ln 43, 46

Stockdale Farm 46
Stonehouse 78
Stonekirk 99
Studrigg Scar **52**
Sulber Gate 55
Sulber Nick 60
Sunbiggin Tarn 6, 81, 87, **92**, 93, 94, 96
Swastika Stone 10, 23, **24**, 25
Swine Tail **57**, 59

Tarn Moor 87
Tarn Sike Beck 94
Thieves Moss 55
Three Greyhounds **99**
Three Peaks 8, 54, 55, 62, 66, 67, 69
Thursgill 90
Toll House, Skipton 10, **30**
Trench Wood 18
Twelve Apostles 10, 22, **24**, 25
Twistleton Scars 62

Victoria Cave 10, 46, 47
Victoria Hall 13, 15, 18

Wandale 91
Wandale Beck 90
Warcop 95
Warrendale Knotts 46
Watlows 45
Wash Dub 51, 52
Weecher Reservoir 17, 18, 19, 22
Weets Top 33, 42, 43, 44
West Fell 81, **85**, 86, 87
Wharfe 49, **51**, 52, 60
Wharfe river 17, 19
Whernside 7, 34, 49, **57**, 62, 65, 66, 67, 69, 82
Whernside Manor 70
Whernside Tarns 67, **70**
Whetstone Gill 42
White Scar Cave 53
White Wells 10, 17, **21**, 22, 23
Wicking Crag 22
Wild Boar Fell 62, 91, **109**
Willy Hall's Spout 23
Winder 65, **74**, 81, 82
Winterburn 33, 39, 75
Winterscales 66, 75
Wold End 65, 67, 70
Wold Fell 67

Yarlside 86

111

Select Bibliography

Stan Abbott & Alan Whitehouse; *The Line that Refused to Die*, Leading Edge (1994)
Keith Boughey & Edward Vickerman; *Prehistoric Rock Art of the West Riding*, WYAS (2003)
David Boulton (Ed); *Adam Sedgwick's Dent*, Hollett & Son (1984)
Stephan Buczacki; *Fauna Brittanica*, Hamlyn (2002)
Andrew Connell; *Appleby Gypsy Horse Fair*, Cumberland & Westmorland A.A.S. (2015)
Eric T. Cowling; *Rombalds Way*, William Walker & Sons (1946)
Paul Ensom; *Yorkshire Geology*, Dovecote Press (2009)
Gary Firth; *A History of Bradford*, Phillimore (1997)
Gary Firth; *Salt & Saltaire*, Tempus Publishing (2001)
John Gooders; *Birds of Britain & Europe*, Kingfisher (1995)
Sheila Gordon; *Lady Anne's Way*, Skyware Press (2012)
Jim Greenhalf; *Salt and Silver*, Bradford Libraries (1998)
Neil Hanson; *Walking through Eden*, Futura (1991)
B.R. Hartley; *Roman Ilkley*, Olicana Museum and Historical Society (2001)
B.R. Hartley & R.L. Fitts; *The Brigantes*, Alan Sutton (1988)
Winifred I Haward; *Yorkshire and the Civil War,* Dalesman Books (1971)
Martin Holdgate; *A History of Appleby*, Dalesman Books (1982)
Martin Holmes; *Proud Northern Lady*, Phillimore (1975)
David Johnson; *Ingleborough, Landscape and History*, Carnegie Publishing (2008)
David Johnson; *Quarrying in the Yorkshire Pennines*, Amberley Publishing (2016)
W.R. Mitchell; *Thunder in the Mountains*, Great Northern (2009)
Arthur Raistrick; *Green Roads in the Mid-Pennines*, Moorland Publishing (1991)
Arthur Raistrick; *Malhamdale*, Dalesman Books (1947)
Arthur Raistrick; *Monks & Shepherds in the Yorkshire Dales*, YDNP Cttee (1976)
Francis Rose; *The Wild Flower Key*, Warne (1981)
Colin Speakman; *Adam Sedgwick, Geologist and Dalesman*, Broad Oak Press (1982)
Colin Speakman; *Walking in the Yorkshire Dales*, Robert Hale (1982)
Ian M. Stead; *British Iron Age Swords and Scabbards*, British Museum (2006)
Paul Sterry; *Complete British Wildlife Photoguide*, Collins (1997)
A Wainwright; *Walks in Limestone Country*, Michael Joseph (1992)
A Wainwright; *Walks on the Howgill Fells*, Michael Joseph (1992)
Tony Waltham; *The Yorkshire Dales Landscape and Geology*, Crowood Press (2007)
Robert White; *The Yorkshire Dales, a Landscape Through Time*, Great Northern (2005)
Clive Woods; *Saltaire – History & Regeneration*, (2000)
Domesday Explorer (CD), Phillimore (2000)

Select Journals & Articles:

The Council for British Archaeology Research Reports; *Gauber high pasture, Ribblehead – an interim report* – Alan King (27, 1978).
Proceedings of the Prehistoric Society; *A New Survey of Ingleborough Hillfort, North Yorkshire* – Bowden M.C.B, Mackay D.A, and Blood N.K. (55, 1989).
Sedbergh Historian; *Sedbergh and the Normans* – Francis Stacey (3,6, 1997); *Cavaliers and Roundheads in Sedbergh, Garsdale and Dent* – Francis Stacey (4,2, 1999); *In the steps of Adam Sedgwick along the Dent Fault* – Denis Sanderson (4,2, 1999);
Yorkshire Archaeological Society Prehistory Research Section Bulletin; *The Ingleborough Hillfort, North Yorkshire* – Alan King (24, 1987); *Rethinking Ingleborough* – Yvonne Luke (44, 2007); *Audit of Archaeological Cave Resources in the Peak District and Yorkshire Dales* – Holderness H, Davies G, Chamberlain A, and Donahue R. (46, 2009).

A number of very useful online resources are also available - please check the *LINKS* section of the *Dales High Way* website **daleshighway.org.uk**